POLANSKI

a biography

the filmmaker as voyeur

Barbara Leaming

SIMON AND SCHUSTER NEW YORK

Published by Simon and Schuster
A Division of Gulf & Western Corporation
Simon & Schuster Building
Rockefeller Center
1230 Avenue of the Americas
New York, New York 10020
SIMON AND SCHUSTER and colophon
are trademarks of Simon & Schuster
Manufactured in the United States of America

10   9   8   7   6   5   4   3   2   1

Library of Congress Cataloging in Publication Data

Leaming, Barbara.
  Polanski, his life and films.

  Bibliography: p.
  Includes index.
  1. Polanski, Roman.   2. Moving-picture producers
and directors—United States—Biography.   I. Title.
PN1998.A3P5825   791.43'0233'0924 [B]   81-16616
ISBN 0-671-24985-1   AACR2

acknowledgments

I would like to extend my gratitude to all who have helped me so generously during the three years I have been working on this project. A book such as this can be written only with the assistance of those willing to share their recollections and perceptions. I interviewed numerous people in America and Europe who have known Polanski at various points in his life and career. A number of them asked that they not be mentioned by name, but I would like to thank at least some of the others who gave me hours of their valuable time: B. H. Barry, Jerzy Bossak, Andrew Braunsberg, Dick Brenneman, Norman Flicker, Roger Gunson, Roman Harte, Barbara Hoff, Adam Holender, Dona Holloway, Ryszard Horowitz, Mieczyslaw Jahoda, Witold Kaczanowski, Bronislaw Kaper, Jerzy Kawalerowicz, Michael Klinger, Henryk Kluba, Michal Komar, Zofia Komeda, Jerzy Kosinski, Diane Ladd, Christine Larene, Grace Lichtenstein, Victor Lownes, Janusz Majewski, Jerzy Matuszkiewicz, Jerzy Mierzejiewski, Janusz Morgenstern, Leopold Nowak, Daniel Olbrychski, Agnieszka Osiecka, Barbara Parkins, Judith Rascoe, Michal Ronikier, Z. Rybarski, Lawrence Silver, Jerzy Skarzynski, Jerzy Skolimowski, Lech Sokol, Joseph Strick, Anthea Sylbert, Richard Sylbert, Waclaw Szaebo, Stefan Szlachtycz, William Tennant, Krzysztof Toeplitz, the late Kenneth Tynan, Wanda Wertenstein, Theo Wilson, and Stanislaw Wohl.

Immediately after deciding to embark on this project, I wrote to Polanski. Neither then, nor on the numerous later occasions when I contacted him, did he agree to be interviewed. However, as far as I know, he never prevented anyone from speaking to me. Thus I have had virtually unlimited access to people without whose cooperation I could not have written this book.

My research for the project has often been extremely

complicated. It involved a great deal of travel, the acquisition of often elusive documentation in several languages, and the viewing of hundreds of hours of film. I had to rely on the willingness of others to facilitate for me everything from travel to film screenings. For the latter I thank the following: MPM Pictures, Paramount Pictures, Films Inc., Audio Brandon, Swank Films, Film Polski, as well as the Polish National Film School at Lodz. I would like to acknowledge my special debt to the late Leszek Armatys, of Filmoteka Polska in Warsaw, who arranged access to one of the most remarkable gifts a biographer of Polanski could receive—a cache of films in which the young Polanski, or "Romek," appeared as an actor. Watching Romek move across the screen gave me a special sense of his past that not even the most vivid personal recollections of friends could have offered.

For their help with significant details of this project, I want to thank Jean-Pierre Jeancolas and Jean Roy, in France; Ewa Siwinska, Elizabeth Bidula and Elizabeth Szczgygielska, in Poland; and Renato Tonelli and Diana Torbarina, in New York.

My agent, Lois Wallace, offered me the initial faith I needed, and continued and unfaltering support throughout. She made numerous perceptive suggestions for improving the various drafts of the book.

Alice Mayhew, my editor at Simon and Schuster, made this book possible by asking the right questions and providing exactly the guidance I needed. Her contribution was immeasurable, and I will always be grateful for her support and encouragement.

Also at Simon and Schuster, the assistance of John Cox and John Herman was endlessly patient and tactful. I also want to thank Vincent Virga, who put together the photo section.

Both Anthony Shiel and Susan Adler read drafts of the manuscript and offered valuable suggestions.

I must also acknowledge the support of my friends in America and Poland, each of whom helped me repeatedly and in ways too varied to enumerate: Gustaw Holoubek, Anya Horowitz, Marysia Konwicka, Antonin Liehm, Yusha

Mehlich, Boleslaw Michalek, Lesley Oelsner, Marek Piwowski and Magdalena Zawadzka.

To my dear friend Elzbieta Czyzewska I owe a very special debt. She consistently shared her insights, made suggestions and stimulated my thinking. I cannot adequately acknowledge her kindness.

Most of all, the writing of this book has taught me a great lesson in intellectual and emotional generosity. Without my husband, David Packman, this book could never have been completed. His willingness to share his ideas and perceptions at every step was the most vital factor of all. He has both my gratitude and my love.

Our kind has no place in the audience. We must perform, we must run the show. If we don't, it's the others that run us. And they don't do it with kid gloves ... Always take care to be sitting on the rostrum and never to be standing out in front of it.

—Mr. Bebra, the midget, to
Oscar, the drummer, in
The Tin Drum by Günter Grass

prologue

A MURDER is about to occur. As the plump, redheaded landlady puts her eye to the keyhole, the camera assumes her
point of view. What we see is framed by the keyhole, which
dissolves after a minute, permitting us to watch the scene
unobstructed. Inside, Alec d'Urberville is at the breakfast
table. As he slices a bit of meat, he is berating Tess, his
tone mocking and sarcastic. He knows that he controls her
sexually, but now she remains cold and impassive. Since
Alec doesn't know that she has just seen the man she loves,
he can't suspect, as we do, that she's about to run him
through with the carving knife. We have witnessed Tess's
meeting with her beloved, so we can interpret her silence.

In his novel *Tess of the d'Urbervilles*, Thomas Hardy
doesn't describe the climactic moment, but we're watching
a film by Roman Polanski, virtuoso of violence, and we
expect him to show all. When Alec rises and moves toward
the door, the landlady pulls away in fear. The moment is
unnerving, for we have nearly forgotten about her and the
keyhole, as we forget about the frame of the screen as we
watch any movie. Reminded of the keyhole, we are impli-
cated as voyeurs; we are caught in the act. Frustrating our
expectations of watching the violent scene, Polanski em-
barrasses us for wanting to see and know things we fear we
should not.

Polanski's films have never been merely about violence.
Like Hitchcock, he is fascinated by the enigma of violence
observed, the special allure of base acts. But Polanski goes
beyond Hitchcock, whose gory masterpieces are made pal-
atable by the ironic distance of the rotund family man, a
director with an impeccable personal life. More is at stake
with Polanski, whose own violent life and times—from Hitler to the Manson "family"—form the subtext of his cinema.

11

Polanski announced his artistic allegiance in the credits of *Repulsion,* his first feature in the West. An eye fills the screen, as the credit title "A Film by Roman Polanski" cuts across it, recalling the razor that slashed the eye in the Luis Buñuel–Salvador Dali surrealist short *Un Chien Andalou.* Buñuel himself wielded the blade in that legendary scene, suggesting the assault perpetrated on the filmgoer's eye, the barrage of shock effects to follow.

While subsequent filmmakers have borrowed the surrealist techniques of *Un Chien Andalou,* they have generally rejected its amorality. Most of the major postwar directors, like Ingmar Bergman, Jean-Luc Godard and Pier Paolo Pasolini, have been moralists. Polanski remains curiously amoral—appealing to dark impulses.

This lack of moral tone, together with the director's painful implication of himself in his work, makes Polanski hard to assimilate in the humanist tradition. Yet, through the libidinous free play of his fantasies, he tells us something about ourselves, inhabitants and victims of a violent time, perversely fascinated by the spectacle of it all. This is why we watch his films, and Polanski.

For Polanski's cinema can't be separated from him. No other major director has theatricalized himself so blatantly —or brilliantly—as when Polanski has recast painful personal events for his films. *Macbeth* (the Manson murders) and *Tess* (the rape case) contain the most obvious examples; *The Tenant,* the subtlest. Increasingly, his cinema has been keyed to the spectator's consciousness of the Polanski image—a life infected by violence and crime. As his image has evolved in the press, he has used it as material in his films, which in turn further shape the image.

Polanski has sought to control his public persona, and his own accounts of his life and work are often unreliable. Still, what Poe called "the imp of the perverse" has frequently caused Polanski to reveal things about himself in his films which he has elsewhere sought to conceal. His often hostile statements in the press indicate what he wants people to think of him, while the films sometimes suggest what he actually thinks of himself.

In my research for this biography, I have spent time in Western and Eastern Europe and in Hollywood—all the places where Polanski has lived and worked—in an attempt to reconstruct the story *behind* the public persona. The name Polanski is itself an artifice, invented by his father, whose real name was Liebling. Wherever Roman Polanski has gone, his name has recalled his Polish roots, his identification with a nation and its culture.

It was in Poland that I turned up the most important clue to Roman Polanski. In Warsaw and Cracow, his old friends referred to him as Romek, the diminutive of Roman. I would ask a question about Polanski, and they would respond by telling me about Romek, the cocky waif and practical joker who somehow evolved himself into the internationally known director and name in the news.

Before he left Poland, Romek was a well-known figure there, a man whose small size and immature appearance tempted friends to treat him as they would a difficult but precocious child. Temperamental, quarrelsome, wildly imaginative and energetic, the Polanski of today is still the Romek they knew in the forties and fifties. (It is no accident that the most disturbing things about the Polanski persona —the amorality, the cruelty, the sexuality—are also the things that disturb us in children.) Polanski's films and scandals are more grandiose versions of Romek's street performances, cruel pranks and early acting roles. On the screen and in the press, Romek has continued to perform, but in the guise of an adult. So, in the end, it is about Romek that I have written this book—the little boy and his dreams, out of which Polanski and his cinema were created.

one

THE SNAPSHOT IS OLD and faded, slightly torn on one side. It was taken in 1946, in Cracow, Poland. Four children appear on a holiday outing to Wawel Castle, the ancestral residence of Polish kings. In the upper right-hand corner a little boy of perhaps six is perched on a stone wall. His slightly parted lips look nervous; traces of anxiety shadow his brow. The child's eyes are dark, vacant and unreadable. The sun is shining, but he is bundled into an oversized woolen topcoat, a heavy muffler tied beneath his chin. The voluminous clothes make him appear even smaller than he is. His ears also seem out of proportion, sticking out from his small head like handles on a jug. With its sharply pointed nose, his pinched, quizzical face might be taken for that of a wizened old man. He looks almost dazed. There is something indefinably eccentric about this child.

Like the seated boy, the two children standing in the foreground bear the mark of some unspeakable horror. The boy, in a sailor suit, is six years old; the girl to his right, seven. A thirteen-year-old girl sits on the wall next to the jug-eared boy.

The quartet is no ordinary group of children on a week-end outing. All four are Jewish survivors of the Nazi holocaust. The two children on the left, Ryszard and Bronislawa Horowitz—brother and sister—have both recently returned from concentration camps. The seven-year-old girl, in a sailor dress, is Roma Ligocka, cousin of the boy in the muffler.

Today, thirty-five years later, the fourth child is immediately, disconcertingly familiar. Wrapped in his coat, which appears too warm for such a sunny day, Roman Polanski gazes into the camera lens. A simple calculation discloses why he looks so peculiar, even in this troubled group of

15

children. This is 1946. Romek, the jug-eared little boy, is not six, but thirteen.

Raymond Polanski—later known as Roman, or the diminutive Romek—was born in Paris on August 18, 1933. His father, Ryszard Polanski, had been living there for several years, working for a record company. A native of Cracow, Ryszard had discarded his original family name, Liebling, and his first wife, whom he had divorced in Poland. In France he met and fell in love with the beautiful Russian Bula Katz. Bula was already married and the mother of a young daughter, but she divorced her husband to marry Ryszard. The Polanskis were living in unluxurious circumstances at number 5, rue Saint Hubert in the XIth arrondissement, not far from the Père-Lachaise cemetery, when their only child was born.

In 1936, Ryszard Polanski returned to Cracow, taking along Bula and three-year-old Raymond, while Bula's daughter from her first marriage, Raymond's half-sister, was left behind. Ryszard's decision to return to his native land was to prove a tragic one.

On September 1, 1939, Hitler's forces invaded Poland. Five days after crossing the Polish frontier, they took Cracow. Romek was six. In the next five and a half years, all but 50,000 of the 3,350,000 Jews living in Poland fled or died. Approximately 4 million people of various races and nationalities perished in the concentration camp at Auschwitz alone. Among them was Romek's mother, who, according to the testimony of a survivor, hurled her eight-year-old son from the truck that was taking her away. This was in 1941, and Romek fled into the ghetto to his father.

There Romek became a smuggler. Smuggling was one of the few ways of getting food and medical supplies in from the outside, and being small, Romek was able to slip through the narrowest fissures in the ghetto wall. Once through an opening, he could pass as any child who belonged outside the wall. At that age Romek did not distinguish a mission from a game, and sometimes he stole out merely in search of stamps for his collection. What would have been foolishly risky to an adult seemed only normally exciting to him.

In 1941, soon after Romek's mother was taken away, his

father was caught in a new roundup of the Jews. However, he had arranged for his son to go into hiding with the family of a Cracow policeman and had provided money for his care. Taking in a Jewish child was punishable by death, but many Poles took the risk.

With both parents gone, so was the child's identity. For most of the occupation, Raymond Polanski was known as Roman Wilk. Wilk, or Wolf, was a suitable name for the little Catholic he would become when, abandoned by the policeman's family, and subsequently by an alcoholic woman who rapidly drank up his remaining money, he was taken in by a peasant family in a village nearby and baptized. He remained in hiding in the Polish countryside until 1945, when he returned alone to Cracow.

By then much of Poland was in ruins. Warsaw had been leveled, reduced to a pile of rubble, but Cracow had been luckier. Its historic buildings had already been fused for explosives, and the Germans were poised to repeat what they had done to Warsaw. But then the Russians surprised them.

Cracow was thus one of the centers of Poland to which the homeless flocked. Conditions turned chaotic as the city's own survivors were joined by refugees from all parts of the country, as well as from other countries of Europe. Nearly everyone seemed to be looking for relatives, and as fate would have it, Romek found his father, a gaunt survivor of Mauthausen, a concentration camp in Austria.

After their reunion, Romek and his father lived for two years in a single room shared with as many as twenty other people. Among them was the Horowitz family, whose children appear in the 1946 Wawel photo. Mrs. Horowitz had been in Mauthausen with Ryszard Polanski. The younger Horowitz child, also named Ryszard, had survived three years of Auschwitz. Despite the difference in their ages (Romek was nearly seven years older), Ryszard and Romek became playmates. With his own mother dead, and his relations with his father deteriorating, Romek attached himself to Mrs. Horowitz.

But Romek could not readjust to the life of a normally obedient son, and it was at this time that Ryszard Polanski, recovering his health, rediscovered his interest in women. When he decided to remarry in 1947, the crisis between him and Romek came to a head.

Ryszard had met Wanda Zajaczkowska while on holiday with the Horowitz family. Wanda was Christian, an outsider to Polanski's circle, an affected blonde who liked furs and flaunted a cigarette holder. She detested Romek. Even the other children could see how badly she treated him, humiliating him at every turn. One friend said angrily, "She treated him like a little Jew boy!" But Wanda was up against an especially difficult child, and she had no idea how to handle him. Romek was so loud and hyperactive that even his father was barely able to tolerate him, screaming on one occasion to a friend of the boy's, "How can you put up with him?" Finally, Wanda issued an ultimatum: Romek would go or there would be no marriage.

Ryszard's decision was a scandal in Cracow. Many of his friends had lost children in the war, and here he was voluntarily giving up a son who had survived. At fourteen the boy was placed in a nearby house as a boarder. His father continued to pay for his support, but he was virtually unsupervised.

From then on, Romek made his own rules, or tried to. He was constantly in trouble. Often he spent the money his father gave him on a childish whim, leaving himself nothing for food and other necessities. His peculiar situation also made him vulnerable in the company with which he chose to mingle. By his own account, he found himself increasingly involved with "delinquents, petty thieves or alcoholics, etc."

Occasionally Romek turned up at the Horowitzes' apartment for a meal or a visit with his friend Ryszard. Mrs. Horowitz found him "disconnected," or forgetful. He seemed now capricious, now preoccupied. On more than one occasion she came out of her kitchen to find that Romek had rearranged the furniture in the other rooms of the apartment.

After some initial tutoring, Romek entered a local technical school to learn electronics. This was an apparent concession to his father, with whom he had fought bitterly over the elder's insistence that the boy prepare for a sensible career and establish an acceptable life-style. But Romek's real interest lay elsewhere. He had joined a children's theater group, working on local radio. Maria Bilizanka, director of the R.T.P.D. theater (Workers Society of Friends of Children), had accepted him as one of her charges when he was twelve. Now, at fourteen, he graduated to the "Merry Group," the child actors who worked on the Cracow radio theater.

One of the boys Romek met in the Merry Group was Renek Nowak. The pair played bit parts together and shared an obsession with the movies, especially the Charles Laughton version of *The Hunchback of Notre Dame*. Romek liked to mimic film characters, and after he and Renek had seen Laughton as the hunchback, he took to lurking in the wings of the darkened theater, dressed as Quasimodo, poised to terrify the prey Renek lured backstage.

Romek also began to imitate the people around him. In doing so, he made an enemy of one of the older actors in the Cracow theater, Josef Karbowski, who was then playing Napoleon in *Madame Sans-Gêne*. The mimicry drove Karbowski to distraction. He had only to see Romek to shout, "You awful little boy!" Romek then dropped his imitation of Karbowski as Napoleon in favor of an imitation of "Karbowski yelling, 'You awful little boy!'"

Romek at this time was fourteen and could not have stood five feet tall, but he insisted on functioning as if he were fully an adult, the equal of his senior colleagues in the Cracow theater. Jerzy Skarzynski, the renowned set designer, said that Romek considered himself already the best actor of any of them. Not surprisingly, Romek's cocky self-assurance and his unsolicited advice got him into constant fights with the others, many of whom were highly skilled professionals. The manager of the theater finally asked Nowak to keep Romek away from the backstage dressing room being used by the others.

But Romek's brilliant gift for mimicry paid off professionally. Still fourteen, he got his first major theatrical part, as a young soldier in the Soviet play *Son of the Regiment*, at the Theater for Young Viewers. The play ran for two years, and Romek won a prize as best actor when it was presented in Warsaw at a festival of Soviet drama.

In 1949, Romek landed another major part, this time as a young clown, a kind of "street urchin," in a play called *Circus Tarabumba*, at the Cracow puppet theater. For the next two years he accompanied the puppets in the play's most important role for a live actor. Obsessed with performance, he became a masterful, if cruel, practical joker, staging epileptic fits and heart seizures for the benefit of the unsuspecting public, principally sedate older women.

But, for Romek, the real show was in the Cracow Market Square. One of the largest squares in Europe, it provides a natural stage. In the center rises the great arcaded Cloth Hall, its parapet demarcated by grimacing stone masks. Around the hall stand a number of cafes. Every day the local populace come to the square to stroll, discuss the news, argue and gossip, or, especially, to see and be seen. Romek began to perform in the square, spinning out stories, cruelly mimicking passersby, attracting attention in whatever way he could. "They hated him in Cracow," said screenwriter Michal Ronikier. "He was little, loud and aggressive." But, whatever the reaction, Romek became a well-known street person, a familiar sight.

Besides performing in the square, Romek had a practical sideline—buying and selling used bicycles and parts. However, it was an enterprise that brought him into contact with some of Cracow's more unsavory types. One day, under the guise of taking him to see a bicycle he could have at a good price, a young hoodlum led Romek to an abandoned German bunker and, inside, knocked him unconscious with a stone. Romek's skull was fractured in the incident, and his watch and money were stolen. Years later he described to friends his vivid memories of how the blood drenched his eyes and how the spray of a shower hitting his face still reminded him of the dripping blood.

In 1950, to his father's dismay, Romek abandoned technical studies and enrolled in art school, the Krakow Liceum Sztuk Plastycznych. A notebook and drawings survive. He had adopted a pseudonym with which he signed most of his artwork—*Dupa*, which in Polish means "bottom," or

"ass." It is also an expletive—an expression of youthful
disdain. The notebook contains, among other things, a
number of childish sketches of female nudes. The most
interesting is of a weeping woman.

Until he entered art school, Romek was inexperienced
with girls. But as that changed, he took up serious body-
building, attempting to develop his scrawny arms and
chest. One curious image in the tattered notebook depicts
a headless male torso. The body is large and heavily mus-
cled, probably a copy from a classical statue rather than
from life. In particular, the genitals are monstrously en-
larged, as if they had been borrowed from a colossus.

Near the headless torso is another image, this one labeled "autoportrait," of a youth whose face bears an unmis-
takable resemblance to a wolf's. Apparently Romek drew
himself as Roman Wilk—Roman Wolf—his wartime identity. But for the boy actually drawing this image, the present also was a turbulent time. For now that he had
discovered sex, he was engaged in his first affair. When he
looked in the mirror and copied what he saw there, Romek
mingled associations of violence and animality.

On the Cracow Market Square there is a stately six-
teenth-century building called the Ram's Palace. Its base-
ment houses Piwnica, the famous satirical cabaret. Romek
began to hang out in the cabaret, and he soon became
wildly infatuated with an actress, slightly older than he,
who performed there. In Cracow the actress from Piwnica
is recalled as Romek's "first big love." Perhaps it was love,
but there is no question that he was cruel to her. On a ski
trip to Zakopane, Romek broke a ski pole over her back
while beating her. Still, for years thereafter, when he met
anyone who knew her, he inquired after her solicitously.

two

ROMEK FINISHED art school in 1953. He had not demonstrated enough talent to justify pursuing art as a career, but the theater offered distinct possibilities. He had accumulated a wealth of experience as an actor and obviously had great potential as a character player—although his range would be limited by his appearance. The state drama school in Cracow had a distinguished reputation, and Romek wanted very much to be admitted.

He prepared for the grueling entrance exams with great seriousness, practicing with a group of other young applicants. All except Romek were subsequently accepted. Polanski recalled much later: "Some of the professors were actors who knew me, and they thought I was too cocky. Already I was quite different from a majority of the applicants, who were scared and running around the corridors of the drama-school with diarrhea and showing all the symptoms of submission and humility. I didn't have any of those symptoms, so they thought I wouldn't be good material to mold, and, thank God, I wasn't, because I would have ended up in some provincial theater in Poland making 2,000 zlotys a month."

After his rejection by the drama school, Romek signed up for a brief stint at the circus academy, where he became involved with a group of inarticulate carnival types, older and even more restless than he. One day Romek, his boyhood friend Adam Holender and several of Romek's circus cohorts were having an outing on a grassy hillside. Romek had been wearing a pair of fancy sunglasses his half-sister had sent him from Paris, and when he removed them and put them down, Holender accidentally sat on them. Furious, Romek summoned his circus friends, who were scattered about, sprawling on the hillside, and demanded that they stage a trial. Led by Romek, they tried, convicted and sentenced Holender to a beating. He was thrust facedown on the ground and whipped with a belt.

Romek didn't stay at the circus academy for long. Renek Nowak had gotten a bit part in a film that was being shot about 125 miles from Cracow. Romek bicycled out to the location, and once there, launched into his familiar antics, starting a fight with Nowak. The director ordered him off the set, but Romek had seen enough to know he wanted to get into films.

An opportunity presented itself that same year. Some film students at the state school in Lodz were preparing to shoot *Three Stories*, a graduation film, and had a minor part for Romek if he wanted it. He did, but first he had to deal with his father. The elder Polanski had never approved of his son's acting on stage and was not about to sanction his becoming a film actor. He refused to believe that Romek had been offered the part, denied him the money to travel to Lodz, and cut off his allowance. The son—he bitterly describes this conflict as the worst in his life—decided to go it alone.

Thus in 1953, at twenty, Romek made his film debut in *Three Stories*—as a boy of about twelve. Before long he was turning up on the screen with regularity and almost invariably as a child. Polanski can be seen everywhere in the Polish cinema of the period. Besides playing in *Three Stories*, he had parts in *The Enchanted Bicycle, An Hour Without Sun, End of the Night, Telephone to My Wife, Lotna, Goodbye Until Tomorrow* and *Innocent Sorcerers*, among others. With few exceptions, his roles were insubstantial.

Still, even these brief parts are interesting on examination because Romek was generally cast as himself: troublemaker, rascal, brat, practical joker—the kid you love to hate. His roles were tinged with childish cruelty, edged with nastiness. He is the loud, bossy ringleader who gets the others into trouble. He is often, as he was in life, the provocateur. And Romek's affinity for provoking violence against himself was a part of it. In 1954 he got a rather good part in *A Generation*, the first feature film directed by Andrzej Wajda, today Poland's best-known director. One of the scenes shows a fight among a group of boys, ending with Romek on the ground being beaten up. The actors had difficulty getting the scene right, and Janusz Morgenstern, who was Wajda's assistant, noticed that in one retake after another the other boys seemed to relish the opportunity of abusing Romek. It was in keeping with the general attitude toward him. Romek's size and his open aggressiveness made him the butt.

In Polanski's early film-acting career, even most of the on-screen jokes were played at his expense. Still, Romek did have a kind of revenge in the film *The Wrecks*. In it Romek is dressed in a torn sweater and jacket, with a schoolbag strapped to his back. The bag conceals a bomb, which he is delivering to a group of wartime resistance fighters. Romek is shown being admitted to an apartment by a beautiful female member of the group. She is in her twenties; he looks about thirteen. He has only a minute or two on screen, enough time to drop off the bomb and leave. First he kisses the woman's hand with exaggerated gallantry, and then he openly leers at her. Quickly, and with no more than a look in his eyes, the boy-man has asserted his sexuality. With calculated audacity, the child has turned lecherous, showing the man trapped in the little boy's appearance.

When Romek finally plays an adult, in *Goodbye Until Tomorrow*, his appearance is part of the plot. The film explores at length the ways in which a small man compensates for his size. A pretty young foreigner catches her first glimpse of Romek and exclaims, "He looks like he's fifteen!" The other characters respond, "He was twenty-six yesterday!" Reacting to this humiliation as in daily life, Romek uses his charm. He shows how well he can dance, how good he is at sports, even that he speaks French. He is not the sort of man who collapses under the weight of embarrassment. Humiliation fuels his need to shine.

Romek eagerly snatched at every opportunity to perform that film gave him, but he quickly discovered that the medium held another appeal as well. The cinema could afford him the possibility of staging his imaginative world, of bringing that world to life for others to see. On the set with Wajda and Poland's other leading directors, he saw that a film actor has only a limited ability to impose his own vision. Ultimately, in the cinema, it is the director who controls the images that appear. So Romek decided to study at the Polish film school at Lodz as a student of directing, while continuing to work as an actor.

He was aware that several factors could militate against his being accepted to the prestigious academy. His father had become moderately successful in a small plastics business, a form of "private initiative" unkindly looked upon by Communist authorities. Moreover, Romek faced a rigorous battery of entrance exams, and his lack of formal education could be a serious handicap. Finally, ever since he had been rejected by the drama school, he had realized how easily he generated personal antagonism, a trait that could go against him with the examiners. In spite of all these anxieties, however, Romek was accepted.

The film school at Lodz is housed in the palace of a prewar merchant prince and is supported by government funds. The Polish film studios and the school were to have been located in Warsaw, but because the capital had been devastated during the war, the film industry and training facilities were "temporarily" set up in Lodz. They are still there. By 1954, when Romek matriculated, Lodz was already one of the finest film schools in the world, although it had been started by the government to create a Polish cinema virtually from scratch. After Stalin's death in 1953, Poland became a place of hope. Its artistic community was aroused by the possibility that real discussion—real communication—would take place once again. In the 1980s the leading force for social change would be the workers. But in the fifties the artists and intellectuals were in the fore. And among the arts, it was film that played the leading role.

Grim though the smokestack-shadowed mill city of Lodz might have seemed, it was one of the best places to be in Poland. The Polish film school had become a remarkable institution—far more successful than most of its Western counterparts. In Lodz the chasm between the film industry and the film academy did not exist, since the working professionals also served as teachers. Many of the best film-makers have taught concurrently with their continuing work in the profession. And even for Lodz, the fifties were something special, a period that would become almost legendary, with the presence of such major figures as Wajda and Andrzej Munk. The Polish filmmakers—both those who were teaching at Lodz and those studying there—were by and large deeply committed to the notion of the public artist. Their principal concern was social rather than solipsistic. Unfettered by the profit motive because the cinema was nationalized, these filmmakers energetically explored the implications of Lenin's dictum that "for us, film is the most important art."

Lodz did not offer opulent budgets or the latest technical equipment. In fact, the palace was rather shabby. Its strength was one of spirit. Film is a collaborative art, and in Polish cinema the potential benefits of collaboration were eagerly pursued at Lodz. There everyone seemed to know everyone else, the film units were developed to provide stable cooperative working groups, and a sense of shared criticism and ideas was emphasized. There was competition but in a positive sense: the achievements of one film-maker spurred another, those of one student, his peers—and the accomplishments of the students became a challenge for their only slightly older professional mentors. The course of study was rigorous: a student had to master every aspect of filmmaking, not just the area in which he had chosen to specialize. The best students were quickly recognized, and they knew that their films were being seen by the very people in whose units they would soon seek employment. In his asocial attitude, Romek was different from the other students, but he was also a product of the special milieu in which he now lived. He benefited as much as anyone from the contact with some of the most vital and rigorous minds in Poland.

Rejecting vapid Stalinist film epics, Wajda's *A Generation* had given life to Polish cinema with a stark portrait of flesh-and-blood young people confronting the problems of living and dying. The atmosphere at Lodz was highly charged with the excitement of a new direction and of the social and aesthetic potential of film. The students at Lodz could even see foreign film, since all films that were sent to Poland for possible distribution were screened there. Most were returned to the West unpurchased and would otherwise have been unseen in Poland.

At Lodz, Romek studied the technical polish of the Hollywood cinema and began to develop a similar style of his own. At the same time, he furthered his skills at self-promotion. Students did their own film projecting in the screening room and thought nothing of running all-night sessions. Access to the room is provided by a broad flight of wooden steps with a landing halfway up. In the fifties, students and instructors would sprawl on the steps to talk feverishly about films being screened upstairs. Romek would position himself on the landing, which set him above and apart, providing an ideal stage for his performance. And although the crowd on the steps usually sat down, Romek always stood.

Agnieszka Osiecka, a poet and playwright, met Romek on the steps to the screening room when they were students at Lodz. She discovered in him a strong need for the public eye and a compulsion to act and entertain. One day he approached the beautiful Agnieszka and invited her to play a game that he used for attracting attention. He would teach her a tongue twister in French and then explain that as they speeded it up, the first one to laugh would be slapped. Since his was the better French, their introduction ended with her being slapped.

A somewhat more pronounced example of his aggressiveness marked Romek's first meeting with Jerzy Kosinski. He poured hot tea on Kosinski's suit. "Why did you do that?" Kosinski asked. "Because I wanted to figure out how someone as well organized as you would react," Romek replied. This was another of Romek's excesses calculated to draw attention to himself, to impose the force of his personality on others, without any thought of consequences.

Romek arrived at a party one night with a book under his arm. Although he was usually boisterous, this time he sank into a chair and began to read as the others were dancing or drinking and chatting. The book, which was French, contained a translation of J. D. Salinger's "A Perfect Day for Bananafish." Seymour Glass, depressed and tempted to suicide, feels comfortable only in the company of little girls, whom he entertains by playing the piano and telling stories. He is given to shocking older women with outrageous remarks. Romek was so engrossed in the tale that he began to read it aloud, translating as he went along. One by one the others stopped to listen. Once again Romek had made himself the center of attraction.

Romek's roommate was a student from Cracow named Janusz Majewski, who is a leading director today, and Majewski was Romek's straight man. He too remarked that Romek couldn't resist performing: the urge might hit him anywhere. A woman was seated opposite the two young men on a bus on their way to school one morning. She seemed tired; possibly she was on her way home from a night-shift. Majewski saw that Romek wanted desperately to catch her attention. His entire body began to shake. From his throat came a loud guttural sound. He dropped to the floor of the bus, pretending an epileptic convulsion.

On another occasion he decided to unsettle one of the film school's secretaries, a staid lady of a certain age. He and Majewski first staged a heated argument in front of her desk. Then Romek whipped out a toy pistol and fired. Majewski fell to the floor. "Polanski has just killed Majewski!" shouted the secretary, hysterically fleeing the scene.

Was there a "real" Romek beyond the childish roles and games? Majewski was as close to him as anyone, and he thought not. Even in the privacy of their room, Romek behaved as if he were on stage. Only when he was depressed was he quiet.

Another student at Lodz, Henryk Kluba, interprets Romek's need to perform in those days "as a protest against the rigidity" of the system. Once Kluba was in a tavern with Romek when there was a power failure. Not only would most of the patrons have been familiar with the repertory of official formula explanations put forth in the event of a failure of any kind, they would also be well schooled in the appropriate responses. The routines were cliché and ponderous. The right routine here would be about mechanical breakdown. In the dark, Romek seized the chance to deliver a most perfunctory explanation. No one could see who was speaking, and Romek was convincing as the voice of officialdom. When the lights came back on, the audience in the tavern broke into applause, never knowing who had made the speech.

At about this time, Romek started attending the jazz sessions at Lodz which had been founded by one of the film students, Jerzy Matuszkiewicz, now a well-known composer. In postwar Poland, jazz was an emblem of personal liberation. The arts had been rigorously restricted under Stalin, and clandestine jazz groups were a means of protest. They met anywhere, even, legend had it, in cemeteries. After Stalin's death, jazz was no longer forbidden, but it had kept its special allure for artists and intellectuals.

The most brilliant of those who came to play at Lodz was a ginger-haired medical doctor from Poznan, Krzysztof Komeda, soon to become the leading figure of Polish jazz and composer for several of Romek's films. Romek was excited by what he heard and saw at the sessions and joined the clique that had formed around Komeda and the other musicians.

Whenever Komeda played in Lodz, his wife, Zofia, would be with him, and it was she who first noticed a "very thin man dressed all in brown" who turned up at every session. No one seemed to know much about this enigmatic fellow, who was noticeable mostly because he always wore a brown suit and was constantly snapping photos. The thin photographer, Jerzy Kosinski, had not yet begun writing novels.

Another figure who seemed always to trail in the shadow of Komeda was an obscure poet, young, pale, very handsome. Soon the others were calling him "Hamlet" because, aside from his beauty, he always dressed in black like his idol Komeda. "Hamlet" was Jerzy Skolimowski, with whom Romek would collaborate on the script for his first feature film, *Knife in the Water*.

Another young habitué of the jazz concerts was fated to play a tragic role in Romek's life. Wojtek Frykowski was the son of a man who was reputed to be the black-market king of Poland. The elder Frykowski was said to control the illegal Polish exchange market in foreign currency, and the son seemed like a Croesus to Romek. He was also drawn to Frykowski's physical strength and muscular appearance. Wojtek was a student at the Polytechnic, not the film school, but he preferred the company of artists. He had everything Romek wanted—money, cars and beautiful women—and he was more than willing to share them with his friends.

Kosinski perceived that Romek and Wojtek "had exactly the same kind of relationship with women." Since both wanted to be worshiped by the opposite sex, young, impressionable girls were most desirable. There is nothing in Polanski of Humbert Humbert's ecstatic adoration of the nymphet; along with Frykowski, his predilection for youth was, from the first, fundamentally narcissistic, basically love of self. One day Kosinski ran into Frykowski when the latter was with a thirteen-year-old girl, Ewa, whom he later married. "Oh my God, is this your sister?" Kosinski asked. "Are you kidding?" Wojtek replied, adding that he had asked Ewa to bring along some of her friends for Romek.

Kosinski felt that Frykowski "worshiped Romek, thinking him 'the most brilliant man ever.' " In return for sharing his wealth and women, the charming but hopelessly untalented Frykowski hoped that some of Romek's aura of the artistic might rub off on him. For Romek had by this time discovered the creative outlet for his pent-up energy. At Lodz—living on a stipend—he learned how to use his fantasies in film and gain attention. He had what one Lodz instructor, Jerzy Mierzejiewski, called "the gift of the nose," a faultless sense of what interests people.

In 1955, Romek began work on his first directing project, a short to be called *The Bicycle*. The subject seemed a natural for him. But whatever happy associations bikes had for him, they also evoked an encounter with violence, the attack in the Cracow bunker. Although Romek struggled with the movie project for two years, *The Bicycle* was never completed.

In 1957, however, Romek managed to complete a modest film, *The Crime*. It offers an odd two-minute glimpse of an apparently unmotivated act of violence. The film begins in shadowy darkness as a door opens into a room where a man lies asleep. Through the door comes a stealthy figure, carrying a knife, which he proceeds to open. He approaches without waking the sleeping man, lifts the knife, stabs the man repeatedly, and departs without a word.

Early viewers of *The Crime* were angered and puzzled. It was scandalous for a student at a state-supported school like Lodz to revel in his private fantasies. But *The Crime* established two key Polanskian obsessions—voyeurism and violence.

In *The Crime*, violence is not subordinated to narrative. There is no moral; the viewer is offered no redeeming social value. Instead, the film operates like the crude pornographic fragments shown before the main feature in a sleazy Times Square theater. While the feature always has a story, or a pretense of one, the preliminary melange of untitled fragments merely plays out a series of sexual obsessions. Although there is no ostensible sex in *The Crime*, it is a pornographic fragment, an exploration of forbidden things, both repugnant and fascinating. The knife enters the victim's body again and again, and the camera accomplishes what the human eye could not: the camera never blinks. This is where the cinema of Polanski differs from Alfred Hitchcock's. When Hitchcock sends the knife down in the famous shower murder sequence in *Psycho*, the film cuts back and forth, preventing a full view of the stabbing. Polanski conceals nothing. His first realized film is a reverie of violence, but it is less the act of violence than the watching of it that fascinates the director.

Next, also in 1957, Romek filmed a three-minute sketch called *Toothy Smile*. In this benign exercise in voyeurism, the camera catches a man descending a staircase in an apartment house. On one landing, he stops to peer through a window at a naked woman taking a bath. When another man, probably her husband, appears from inside the apartment, the Peeping Tom departs. But he is soon compelled to return, and this time, to his consternation, he finds the husband instead.

In his next film, *Break Up the Ball*, made in 1958, Romek

once more indulged his impulse to voyeurism. This time the violence was real, actually planned by the director so that he might film it.

Romek had first arranged to film the annual student dance at Lodz. Then he had invited a group of local toughs to "show what they could do." On the appointed night the toughs arrived and beat up the unsuspecting students. Romek filmed the scene from behind the safety of his camera. No wonder he counts among his favorite movies. Michael Powell's *Peeping Tom,* a tale about a murderer who films his victims as he kills them, in order to record their fear. The curious project outlined in Powell's film was, in a sense, Romek's own in *Break Up the Ball*—to provoke fear, then to record it.

Romek had had no trouble recruiting the hoodlums, for he himself was well known in Lodz as a tough. One of his exploits, in a tawdry bar in Lodz, had become legendary. A local thug who hung out in the bar had beaten up one of Romek's friends. It so happened that, at the time, Romek had a broken arm, and it was encased in a heavy plaster cast. In spite of his injury, upon hearing about his friend, he stormed off to the bar to confront the assailant. "Which of you beat up one of my men?" he snapped on entering the bar. A voice was heard from a gang of toughs: "It was me, and what are you going to do about it?" "I'll break your jaw!" Romek shot back as the smirking tough stepped before him. Then, the legend has it, with all the force he could muster, Romek swung the leaden cast and shattered the man's jaw. After that, Romek's reputation was secure in the lower depths.

Appropriately, in his next short, Romek played a thug, the unsavory-looking leader of a sinister gang of youths. *Two Men and a Wardrobe* chronicles the absurd journey of two men lugging an enormous mirrored armoire on an itinerary completely without rationale. Actually, the absurdity is a superb cinematic device that permits the camera to explore the strange scenes through which the travelers pass. At one point, the two men run into Romek and his gang. For no apparent reason, Romek strikes one of the travelers.

The film is shot through with gratuitous violence. Even before the thugs accost the two men with the wardrobe, Romek and company are seen stoning a tiny kitten. This sequence led to a controversy during the filming when a woman from a Polish humane society happened upon the location and demanded that the sequence be halted. She furiously upbraided the nonchalant director and subsequently registered a complaint at the film school.

In perhaps the most unsettling episode in *Two Men and a Wardrobe*, a young man is beaten to death by a rock-wielding assailant and his head is thrust into the water of a stream, thereby mingling blood and water as in the director's recurrent fantasies of his own early traumatic experience in the Cracow bunker. This would become an important tendency in Polanski's career—to respond to the chaos and violence of his personal experience with cinematic mastery of them. It is generally overlooked that the director here was actually turning the tables, the victim of cruelty becoming its imaginary perpetrator by staging scenes of violence he both identified with and controlled.

Shooting on *Two Men and a Wardrobe* was constantly held up by Romek's fits of rage, thus establishing his reputation as a brutal and temperamental director. Frequently when the filming didn't go exactly as he wanted, Romek took a punch at the armoire's mirror, so that the crew had to replace the shattered glass several times. Henryk Kluba, who played one of the two men of the title, found the director's performance at once "comic and grotesque." Romek was given to storming off the set in tantrums, leaving both crew and actors confounded, then reappearing, as if nothing had happened, and resuming command.

Passionately concerned with his image, Romek took to dressing elegantly for appearances on the set, in dramatic contrast to the hoodlum getup he wore on screen. Once, while directing, he changed outfits four times in a single day.

From the start, Romek had bragged that his film would win first prize at the international short-film competition at the 1958 Brussels Worlds Fair. In the end, it won only third place, but that was enough to give him some leverage back in Poland. Romek was invited to Brussels with the Polish delegation to accept his prize. His diminutive size and boyish face caused almost as much stir there as his film.

Back at school, Romek completed two more student projects. The first, *The Lamp*, in 1959, depicts the plight of a dollmaker whose shop goes up in flames owing to faulty wiring in its newly installed electrical system. It is a failed exercise, which Polanski frequently omits from his filmography. The second, notwithstanding Polanski's fractiousness at being treated like a student after his success abroad, is a stunning graduation film, *When Angels Fall*, in which he makes an odd cameo appearance disguised in drag. Polanski's first work in color, it is the story of a wrinkled old woman who attends a men's public lavatory. Superbly played by a nonprofessional whom Romek had discovered in an old-age home, the attendant seems oblivious to the gurgling in the urinals or toilets as countless men relieve themselves directly in front of her or in the cubicles to one side. Sitting day after day, she slips into reveries of her lost soldier love and the child she bore him—scenes rendered in lyrical flashbacks and in stunning counterpoint to the mocking assignations being played out in the toilet.

In the earliest flashbacks, the woman in youth is played by an actress who had become Romek's companion of the period, Barbara Kwiatkowska. Peering out through a window when we first see her, Kwiatkowska is the essence of ripe, sensuous young womanhood. Her thick hair is twisted in long braids, her eyes are enormous; but her most striking aspect is her mouth, with unbelievably full, pouting lips. Romek, ever fascinated by the idea of violence observed, has his beauty gazing out in perplexity at a cruel little boy beating a helpless frog with a switch.

When Angels Fall is riddled with such crudity and cruelty. To date, it is the only one of Polanski's works that deals directly with the brutal absurdity of wartime experience, something Romek knew well. Perhaps the film's most curious moment is another flashback in which the woman, somewhat older than before, is played by Romek himself. Like his prior work at its most audacious, this was, for Romek, a masquerade, a means of both baring and concealing himself.

It is unfair to evaluate most artists' juvenilia in relation to their mature work. But Polanski is an artist of immaturity who has not outgrown the cruelty and amorality of his earliest films. His technical skills have become more refined; his work has acquired the veneer of the accomplished craftsman. Still, Romek's juvenilia provides a glimpse of the most elemental force in Polanski's cinema, his preoccupation with voyeurism and violence.

three

WHEN ROMEK'S COMPANION Barbara Kwiatkowska appeared
in his graduation film, she was already a well-known actress in Poland. She had gotten her start in 1957, when one
of the weekly picture magazines held a contest to "Get
Beautiful Girls on Screen!" The contest was an index of the
increased desire to emulate things Western which followed
the Polish October of 1956. Criteria like talent and training,
more traditional for a Polish film actress, were not considerations in this contest; basic good looks were the sole re-
quirement. The prize was to be a starring role in a feature
film. When the results were announced, Barbara Kwiatkowska—or Basia, as friends called her—had won: an un-
trained seventeen-year-old country girl from the village of
Szulechow.

Basia's film debut was in a deft comedy called *Eve Wants
to Sleep*. Directed by Tadeusz Chmielewski, it concerns a
naive country girl in the big city, a perfect role for the wide-
eyed beauty-contest winner. As the innocent Eve, Basia
was an overnight sensation, becoming Poland's first
Western-style movie starlet. Established professionals in
her new field, however, were not always enthusiastic about
what Basia represented. For them she was not a real actress, one who had taken the heretofore obligatory route to
the screen via drama school and theatrical experience. Instead, her success was based solely on her physical appearance and the Western glamour it hinted at. Suddenly, as
the result of a contest and a film, post-Stalin Poland had a
symbol of the sophistication it desired, ironically in the
form of this young and innocent beauty.

Romek met Basia while she was making her second film,
1000 Thalers [*Tysiac Talarow*]. His friend Henryk Kluba
had worked as Chmielewski's assistant, preparing Basia for
her screen test. When she and Romek met, Basia was only

eighteen, seven years younger than he was. Still unspoiled by her instant success, still a charming country girl at heart, she was impressed and amused by Romek's antic behavior and easy patter. Kluba felt that Romek dominated her from the start, the opportunist utilizing his superior intelligence and his experience. Romek was driven, Kluba thought, by a profit motive, a desire to be seen with the star for whatever advantage that might accord him. Methodically, he pursued her, undaunted by his student status. "It was very elegant to be in love with her," said Agnieszka Osiecka. "So, for Romek, having this girl was quite something— from the point of view of ambition." When Basia was sent to the film festival at San Sebastian in Spain to accompany *Eve Wants to Sleep*, Romek turned up there, much to everyone's surprise—and no mean feat for a penurious student. Through Basia, he mingled with members of the international film festival circuit, who were charmed by the teenaged star from Poland.

Basia replaced Janusz Majewski as Romek's roommate in a tiny flat near the radio station in Lodz. It was expected that Basia would embrace the life-style of Romek and his circle. Nevertheless, the fact that he was cohabiting with the first real star of the Polish cinema lent him considerable status with his student friends. Although he was still appearing regularly in his characteristic little boy roles in films, he was the senior and controlling member of his relationship with Basia. But his situation also led to cruel jokes at his expense. Some people called him "Mr. Kwiatkowski."

In 1959, Romek and Basia were married. The wedding was quick and without formality or ritual. Krzysztof and Zofia Komeda, the first guests to arrive for the "reception," were startled to find that no preparation had been made for the guests. What festivities and refreshments there were were improvised on the spot by Zofia.

Romek and Basia's marriage was a wildly erratic affair: one moment Romek was ecstatic, the next enraged. His moods could shift with astonishing speed, as his friend Adam Holender, by now also a film student, witnessed one night. The two students were on an evening train, returning to Lodz from Warsaw. Romek spent the entire ride describing the wonders of Basia and marriage. Romek never felt comfortable explaining something in words alone, so soon he was insisting that the still-unmarried Holender come and see for himself this miraculous new world of Romek's—that very night. Holender hesitated: when the train arrived at ten-thirty, it would be awfully late to drop in on Basia unannounced. Romek insisted. By the time they got to the young couple's building, Romek was practically beside himself with excitement. He flew up the stairs in anticipation of seeing his bride. He embraced Basia ardently, almost swooning in his passion. Then, without a second of transition, the gears switched: Romek wanted to eat.

Romek and Holender sat down, and in moments the gears switched again when Basia dropped an egg on the floor. Romek looked at the shattered egg, then at Basia, his love replaced by cold rage: "You stupid idiot!" he screamed. "You clumsy—" The scene was typical of their relationship. Rage could overwhelm Romek as easily as love, just as his attention could be diverted the moment an opportunity cropped up to gain the spotlight.

The latter was never more obvious than one night when Romek and Basia went to a local ballroom in Lodz. Romek was dancing with Basia in his usual ostentatious way when suddenly he noticed that his former roommate, Majewski, had come into the hall. At the time, Majewski had the reputation of being the best dancer in Lodz. Romek paused for a moment, then turned, and left Basia in the middle of the floor. He strode over to Majewski, and without a word, the two men began to dance together.

Shortly after his wedding, Romek received his directing diploma from the film school and was assigned to the KAMERA unit, the filmmaking group headed by his former instructor Jerzy Bossak. Bossak made him an assistant to the great Polish director Andrzej Munk. A new film, to be called *Bad Luck*, was in the planning stages, and Munk was searching for actors. In a Warsaw film journal, Romek wrote an article in which he described the difficult search for an actress to play one of the roles: "a girl with good manners and a soul steaming with ugliness and sin."

Basia was eventually selected for the part of Jola, a nymphet whose innocent exterior conceals something deeply erotic. With Basia cast, Munk decided to have some fun and cast Romek in the part of the tutor she seduces. Through an illuminated window, student and tutor are glimpsed embracing, while the girl's parents assume they are studying.

Basia's career as an actress was by then in high gear in Poland. Since she wasn't tied down to drama school or the theater, she was one of the few young actresses readily available to Polish film directors. Only yesterday an obscure country girl, today she found herself working with the top movie directors in the country. She was most content with her good fortune, but Romek had other ideas. In 1960 a phone call came to Kwiatkowska from Paris. By chance, Romek answered. A French producer had seen *Eve Wants to Sleep* at a festival and wondered whether Kwiatkowska would be interested in making a French film. Before Romek could say anything, the caller added, "Can she speak French?" *"Bien!"* ("Well!"), replied Romek, who quickly maneuvered himself an invitation to Paris as Basia's husband, language coach and general manager. When he hung up, he announced the news to Basia. As both well knew, Basia didn't speak a word of French.

When news of the Polanskis' impending departure hit the gossip mills of the Polish film community, the familiar jokes about "Mr. Kwiatkowski" were given another run, and there was widespread speculation that the aggressive, self-seeking Romek would destroy Basia's career once they got to the West. But the trip was a success for her, after an awkward beginning. When the producer met with the Polanskis, he attempted to talk to Basia, only to encounter blank incomprehension. Obviously there had been some misunderstanding. Certainly Basia was even prettier than he had hoped, but hadn't he asked M. Polanski if his wife spoke French? And hadn't M. Polanski replied, *"Bien"?* "Oh, no!" M. Polanski exclaimed, slapping his head with his palm. The producer must have misunderstood. M. Polanski had said, *"Rien!"* ("Not at all!").

Having paid their way to Paris, the producer was easily

convinced that letting them stay made sense financially. Romek would teach Basia her lines for *1000 Windows*.

Romek even invented a new name for his wife's debut in French cinema. There was at this time a popular French actress, Marie Laforêt, whose name reminded Romek of the Polish word for "forest," which is *las*. He then learned that the addition of another "s" would mean "young woman" or "girl" in English, and he thereby hit upon the new name he sought—Barbara Lass.

Romek had come to Paris interested in more than coaching and promoting Basia. His friends in Poland knew that he had gone abroad intending to court the financing that would enable him to make his first feature film in the West. Here he differed from most other Polish directors of the period, who desired success abroad in order to re-enforce their status at home. Foreign recognition was part of the power game in the Polish film milieu. Western prizes and critical acclaim were much coveted. But Romek wanted something more—he wanted to become a Western director. The fortuitous invitation to Basia provided the longed-for chance to hustle on behalf of his own projects.

Although *1000 Windows* was an undistinguished film, Basia—now Barbara Lass—was a hit with French filmgoers. She acquired an agent to handle the offers that came in to cast her in more films. Romek, however, could not get the backing needed to shoot a feature. Big-time French producers weren't interested in unproven Lodz graduates.

Romek confided his humiliation to a male friend. It had crystallized, he said, one afternoon when he found himself waiting outside an elegant Parisian hotel. Basia was upstairs with film director René Clément, who would soon feature her, opposite Alain Delon, in *Quelle joie de vivre*. Clément's expensive sports car was parked near the hotel entrance, and Romek stared at it enviously.

While in Paris, Romek was interviewed by the French film journal *Positif* concerning the prize-winning *Two Men and a Wardrobe*. Romek described an idea for a new film: "... it will be the story of a young girl attracted by the mirage of the cinema and who wants at all cost to become a star." The concept may have reflected his anxieties about

Basia, but he did not get to make the feature about the ambitious girl.

However, Romek finally did obtain financing for a fourteen-minute short, *The Fat and the Lean*, which he co-directed with Jean Rousseau. The film opens with a tiny barefoot slave—portrayed by Romek—playing a flute and beating a drum while his counterpart, the gargantuan master—the late French actor André Kattelbach—rides a broken-down rocking chair on the lawn in front of a crumbling mansion. With increasing frenzy, Romek begins to leap and pirouette, dancing for his master like a harlequin gone mad. In seconds he manages to delineate a character. Wiping Kattelbach's sweaty brow, feeding him, washing his feet, shading him from the sun with an enormous umbrella, even holding a urinal for him—he is the perfect slave, as eager to debase himself as to please. That the slave comprehends, even identifies with, the master's brutality is suggested when, momentarily tied to a goat, he kicks the beast cruelly, thereby assuming the role of aggressor. *The Fat and the Lean* is Polanski's first explicit comment on the mechanisms of power and humiliation, the strange symbiosis that joins master and slave.

Despite its austere beauty and penetrating psychological insight, Romek's first Western film was initially unsuccessful, nearly landing the small French company that financed it in bankruptcy. In time, *The Fat and the Lean* garnered the prizes and acclaim it deserved, but Romek needed the recognition now, in 1961, and it was not forthcoming.

After eighteen months in Paris, Romek and Basia realized that their marriage was disintegrating. She was working steadily, making films, while Romek seemed unable to score the commercial success he dreamed of. The decision to separate was made: Basia would remain in Paris to work, and Romek would return to Poland. He would do so driving a fire-engine-red sports car recently purchased with his wife's film earnings.

Back in Poland, the flashy convertible enabled Romek to pretend he had achieved wealth and success. With the top rolled down, he picked up Jerzy Skolimowski and his wife and their dog, for a breakneck tour of Warsaw—mostly to show off the car, which he parked for public display in front of S.P.A.T.I.F., the actors' club. To conceal the frustration and embarrassment he was feeling and forestall speculation that all had not gone well abroad, Romek regaled his Warsaw cronies with news of the latest Western trends in film and fashion. He even demonstrated the new dance fad, the twist. But his real plight quickly became obvious to everyone. He had lost his bride in Paris.

The harshest verdict was rendered by Henryk Kluba: "Polanski fell in love with Kwiatkowska at the moment he lost her." Soon word drifted back to Poland that Basia was seriously involved with another man, the handsome German actor Karl Heinz Boehm, the star of one of Romek's favorite films, *Peeping Tom*. But Romek's breakup with Basia was not merely a question of conflicting ambitions, as he seemed to have construed it. On the contrary, she confided to a friend, Basia had come to realize that "Romek would always be difficult." She wanted a dependable husband and a family, a life different from anything she could have expected with Romek.

In time, Basia moved to divorce Romek so that she might marry Boehm, but Romek resisted. Although he had agreed to leave her in Paris, he was not about to give her up for good without a struggle. The divorce could not be obtained without Basia's returning to Poland. Basia was aware of the kind of pressure Romek could exert if she had to confront him alone. So when "Barbara Lass" returned to Poland for a divorce, it was with Boehm at her side.

Their visit was the talk of Warsaw. When they arrived at a late night party, the attention of everyone there turned to the glamorous couple, whose obvious affluence labeled them unmistakably as visitors from the West. In contrast to Basia and her dashing German fiancé, the others at the party looked provincial. Basia and Boehm were dressed to the teeth, aware of the power game to be played. Still poor, shabbily dressed, and with only a few short films to his credit, Romek was no match for them. Ultimately, he had no choice but to give up his attempt to prevent the divorce.

After Basia married Boehm, one of Romek's friends said: "I had a feeling that he was deeply humiliated by Basia. I mean by the divorce and the movie star and his being a

short man and Basia's being tall and young and beautiful."
In years to come, the press seemed to be able to get Polanski to talk about almost any subject, but two were off limits
—his mother and Basia.

four

ALTHOUGH DEPRESSED by Basia's decision, Romek had reapplied himself to his directing career. His return to Poland had been spurred partly by a letter from Jerzy Bossak, urging him to revive a script proposal begun with Jerzy Skolimowski before the abortive trip to Paris: "What are you doing sitting there in France?" wrote Bossak, convincing Romek that he must try again with his and Skolimowski's ambitious concept for *Knife in the Water*. Bureaucratic pressures had blocked production before. Back in Poland, Romek tried again to persuade the authorities to approve and finance the film.

The initial collaboration with Skolimowski had been a volatile one, their interplay productive but fraught with conflict. Skolimowski had burst on the Polish artistic scene with the flashiest of entrances. An artist with a genius for self-promotion that rivaled Polanski's, Skolimowski had carefully plotted his road to success. Figuring that the most rapid way to recognition was as a poet, he had managed to publish two slim books of angry verses and had gotten himself admitted to the Polish Writers Union—as its youngest member, aged twenty-three. With his writers' union card in his pocket, Skolimowski then took himself to the country estate run by the union as a retreat for its members, there to see whom he could meet.

Not only was Skolimowski witty and clever, he was capable of seizing ideas and developing them with great speed. He was also delicately handsome, and to make sure that no one called him "sissy," he had learned to box and sported a broken nose to prove it—a feature that made him look like a kind of Pre-Raphaelite thug.

At the writers' retreat when Skolimowski arrived were Jerzy Andrzejewski, one of the most famous postwar novelists, and Andrzej Wajda. Novelist and director were work-

44

ing on a film script about the younger generation—
Skolimowski's own. The poet began to listen in as they
talked. Soon he dared make suggestions, and when they
were well received, a few more. Before long, Skolimowski
had become Andrzejewski's protégé and his coscenarist for
Wajda's *Innocent Sorcerers*. Skolimowski then made an
enormous leap. When the film began shooting, he had been
cast in the most erotically charged part, the brutalized
boxer. Like Romek, Skolimowski was passionately ambitious, constantly devising new strategies for making it.

Romek and Skolimowski first met casually at the Lodz
jazz sessions, but they became "partners" when Skolimowski decided to take the entrance exams for film school.
Romek was about to graduate and was helping the professors administer the exams. Skolimowski treated it as certain
that he would be accepted—after all, he had already co-
authored a script for Wajda. Romek was attracted by Skolimowski's assurance, and they went on to become good
friends.

Romek had been struggling at the time—it was 1959—to
come up with a project for his feature-directing debut and
asked for Skolimowski's help on the script, a two- or three-
character drama set in the Mazurian lake district of Poland.
While there once, Polanski had shared a girlfriend with an
older man, a sailor, who took every chance to humiliate his
rival. Experience of the erotic triangle had given Polanski
his initial idea for the script.

In the midst of a heat wave, Polanski and Skolimowski
had secluded themselves in a tiny, sweltering apartment to
write. They were joined by Romek's elfin friend Jakub
(Kuba) Goldberg. Although Goldberg would receive a
screenwriting credit, and undoubtedly contributed some
ideas, Skolimowski claims that he "didn't write a single
word"; his job was to run cold water in the bathtub to cool
the writers' drinks, as ice was a luxury beyond their means.
Romek, Skolimowski recalls, "liked having Goldberg
around because he was shorter." Today, Skolimowski says
that when they "were younger and more immodest," he
and Romek would claim that the writing of *Knife in the
Water* took only three days. Now, he chuckles, he would
admit to four.

In the apartment, time was the first topic discussed: Romek's original idea called for a narrative spanning several days. Skolimowski, however, sought a rigorous temporal unity. On this, Romek deferred to Skolimowski, agreeing to limit the events to a single twenty-four-hour period. Next, the pair set about enumerating the details of the plot and defining the characters, acting out all the parts and assuming the various personalities and sexes. They took turns playing the middle-aged man, his pretty wife and a young male hitchhiker they pick up on their way for a day of sailing. This method led the two writers to explore and eventually comprehend the dynamics of role playing, the games of domination and submission, depicted in *Knife in the Water.*

But exacerbated by the heat and the claustrophobic conditions of the wretched flat, the psychological strains of their encounter led to open conflict. Acting out and developing the roles of the story's sadomasochistic characters, Polanski and Skolimowski quarreled bitterly, each struggling for power in their working relationship. Skolimowski speculated later that only because he was a boxer was he spared actual violence, so enraged did Polanski become. As it was, Polanski resorted to what Skolimowski found "unbearable" shrieking, desperately badgering his collaborator. "But I'm the prize-winning filmmaker!" he screamed, referring to his third place at Brussels for *Two Men and a Wardrobe.* "But I'm the writer!" Skolimowski shouted back, waving his union card. Meanwhile, a script was actually being written, with Skolimowski rapidly jotting down the lines and action as they were developed.

When the completed script was submitted to Jerzy Bossak for consideration by his film unit, it was approved immediately, only to be rejected at a higher governmental level. This politically aloof psychological drama was not the sort of film the Polish State wished to spend its money on. The script's lack of overt political subject matter rendered the project threatening. And Polanski did not have the leverage of a name or personal prestige that might gain a tested feature director some acceptance by the bureaucracy.

During Romek's frustrating sojourn in Paris, Skoli-

mowski had kept at the script they had written, painstakingly reworking its dialogue. Thus, when Romek returned
to Poland, encouraged by Bossak, there was a fresh project
to be taken up. Polanski revised the script himself, in light
of new ideas he had, and the result, very different from the
original, was then resubmitted to the authorities for their
consideration.

But the decision was slow in coming, and anxious to
work, Romek launched into another project—a short film
called *Mammals*, based on a script he had written with his
friend from Lodz, the future director Andrzej Kondratiuk.
Its slight plot is a variant of the master-slave theme of *The
Fat and the Lean*. In *Mammals* two men trudge through a
snowy landscape, alternately pulling one another on the
sled they share and maneuvering to control it. At times,
wrapped in white bandages, the figures merge with their
snowy environment, making them momentarily indistin-
guishable from it. Finally they become so engrossed in
their struggle that someone else manages to steal the sled,
the vehicle of their ludicrous power game.

Polanski proposed the idea for *Mammals* to the
SEMAFOR short-film studios. But SEMAFOR expressed
reservations: Was the snow necessary? After all, at the moment there wasn't a trace of snow to be found except in the
mountains. And going on location would be too expensive.
Polanski was adamant, refusing to alter the script and the
snow it called for to suit financial constraints. Instead—
incredibly—he devised a means to shoot his film in the
precise way he wanted, by financing it with independent
money, a notion absolutely undreamed of in Poland, where
the cinema is nationalized. Polanski's money-man, or producer, was Wojtek Frykowski, who also managed to play a
small role in the film, as the rogue who steals the sled.

Learning of Polanski's scheme, people gasped at his audacity. In securing private financing, Polanski was definitely thinking Western-style. As with *Two Men and a
Wardrobe*, he embarked on his project with a festival prize
in mind, explicitly seeking to shore up his position in Poland with Western recognition. In the end, *Mammals* won
two awards—at Tours in France and Oberhausen in Germany. In Poland, despite the highly irregular situation of

the film's private financing, SEMAFOR eventually bought it from Polanski and Frykowski for release through official channels.

While still working on *Mammals*, Polanski received word that the script for *Knife in the Water* had been approved. Bossak, as head of KAMERA, had thrown his considerable prestige behind the project, giving it the clout Romek himself did not yet have. By then, *Mammals* had been shot but not edited. The project was temporarily put aside so that Polanski could begin preparations for his feature debut.

Knife in the Water was to be filmed on location at the Mazurian lakes. First, cast and crew needed to be assembled. In particular, the director was concerned with precisely how his film would be shot, seeking a visual equivalent for the states of mind registered in the script. Polanski brought in as director of photography one of Poland's most experienced, Jerzy Lipman, who would prove invaluable to the young director in solving technical problems caused by the confined dimensions of the boat and the constantly shifting light of the lake's surface. Under Lipman, Polanski placed his old friend from Lodz, Andrzej Kostenko, who had worked with him on *Mammals*. Polanski discerned that Kostenko's experience shooting in the glare of the snowy locale of that film would serve him well on this new project, where the lake posed equally formidable difficulties. The director would have his cameraman use the play of light and reflection to create the painfully claustrophobic space in which the film's psychological conflict occurs.

Because the drama had only three characters, casting was especially important. The role of the husband was the only one filled by a professional. Leon Niemczyk was cast as the vain, acquisitive, aging husband troubled by the loss of youth. Niemczyk's highly polished speech would be in character with the slightly too-smooth sports journalist he was to portray and would contrast vividly with the less confident manner of the two younger characters, the journalist's wife and the boyish hitchhiker.

To find someone to play the wife, Polanski began to haunt the trendiest Warsaw swimming pool, a logical place to look for a girl who would spend much of her time on screen in a bikini. After inspecting numerous female bodies, Polanski settled on a pretty music student named Jolanta Umecka. The girl, Henryk Kluba saw at once, bore a striking resemblance to Romek's ex-wife, Basia Kwiatkowska. For Polanski, looks were more important for this role than acting ability or experience, both of which Umecka lacked. As a director, Polanski is known for his contempt for actors and for his confidence that he can wrest a performance from anyone. As Skolimowski would say, if people needed proof of how good a director Romek was, Umecka's performance on screen provided it.

A single part remained to be cast. According to Polanski and Skolimowski's concept, the hitchhiker was to be young and handsome, sexual in a way that is clearly threatening to the aging husband. During preparations for the film, it seemed odd to those around him that Polanski did not seem to have anyone under consideration for this key role. Soon they learned why: Polanski had decided to play the part himself.

With only a week left before the scheduled start of shooting, Bossak decided to intervene. He called Polanski in to KAMERA's production offices and straightaway asked who would play the young man. "I will!" Romek announced. Bossak knew that there was no time to worry about wounded feelings. So he told Polanski that, as head of the unit, he refused even to consider the idea. Polanski simply did not have the necessary looks.

Polanski shot Bossak a furious glance, proclaiming that either he would play the part or no one would. Who was Bossak to tell him that he wasn't attractive enough? But Bossak stood firm. There was, he said, no possibility of further discussion. The choice was not Polanski's to make. Either Polanski would cast another actor or the film would be canceled. Polanski stormed out of the office.

Five minutes later, the door flew open and in stomped Polanski again—stark naked. "Now, am I not handsome enough for the part?" he demanded, positioning himself in front of Bossak. Glancing at the naked figure and then away, Bossak replied quietly, "First, you and I are both normal men. Put on your clothes, or there will be all sorts of gossip about us. Second, you are *not* going to play the part, so cast it immediately, or we will put off the film until next year."

Dressed again, Polanski began thinking about actors. But, for him, whatever actor it might be would be only his stand-in, for he felt that the part was rightfully his. To play the hitchhiker, Romek now proposed his lean, blond collaborator, Skolimowski. A screen test was arranged, but in spite of the writer's striking appearance and acting ability, the results were disappointing.

Finally, Polanski chose an acting student from Lodz named Zygmunt Malanowicz. The handsome Malanowicz bore no resemblance to Polanski and, with his dark hair, didn't seem to look much like Skolimowski either. But, in choosing Malanowicz, Polanski's eyes were more acute. Assisted by a bottle of peroxide, as called for by Polanski, Malanowicz acquired blond hair. Suddenly he looked a lot like Skolimowski, as he does in the completed film. As for Polanski, he too is oddly present in the role of the hitchhiker, for it is his voice we hear speaking the lines: Romek dubbed the hitchhiker's voice with his own.

Now at last, cast and crew took off for the location at the Mazurian lakes. Driving there at top speed, in the company of Kuba Goldberg, Polanski wrecked his automobile, the first of many such accidents during shooting. Arriving on the set, Romek laughed about the accident, making it into a joke at the expense of Goldberg's size: "Kuba," he announced, "fell into the ashtray."

On the set, Polanski seemed to zero in on his actress, Jolanta Umecka, who became the target of open bullying and abuse. Romek's discovery at the swimming pool grew so tense and distraught that she began to stuff herself with sweets and was soon bursting out of her tiny bikini. Off the set, Polanski is said to have told Umecka that he had fallen in love with her. But their ensuing affair was a cruel prank. After each tryst with Umecka, Polanski would report the details to the boys, who would offer suggestions on his next moves on the unsuspecting actress. Their most private embraces were often furtively observed—with Romek's connivance—by those in on the joke.

The controversy surrounding official approval to shoot *Knife in the Water* did not cease once filming began. Ac-

cording to one observer, the critic and screenwriter Boleslaw Sulik, rumors began to circulate about sexual "orgies"
taking place on the location. Sulik says that this almost
caused the film to be shut down, until the rumors were
shown to be "unfounded." Still, the air of controversy
caused some journalists to suspect that a good story might
be found here. Newsmen turned up to see what Polanski
was doing and sent back reports that the film was not "serious" enough, a damning suggestion in politically conscious Poland.

Unlike Polanski, Bossak was acutely sensitive to the potential for political scandal. Having initially sponsored the
project, he wanted it to work. On a trip to the lakes, he
looked at the rushes and discovered that Polanski was
using a Mercedes-Benz for the automobile sequences.
Even a seemingly innocuous detail like an expensive car
could raise the ire of the censors in Poland. Realizing the
Mercedes connoted a kind of ostentation—even decadence
—that would needlessly provoke official wrath, Bossak suggested to Polanski that it would be more discreet to use a
modest Peugeot. The director began to yell, shrieking that
it was *his* film and that he absolutely insisted upon the
Mercedes. "I am sorry," said Bossak, "but your film is generally not very well accepted with the authorities. To have
a Mercedes would be to have additional trouble. You must
change it." As Bossak recalls, Polanski went "crazy." Deciding to give him time to cool off, Bossak returned to his
hotel, leaving word that Romek should come to see him
there in an hour. Although Polanski finally deferred to the
idea of the Peugeot, only the exteriors were reshot. The
already completed interior shots of the Mercedes were retained.

Precisely why was *Knife in the Water* such a controversial project? The completed film best answers the question.
Like his earlier shorts, Polanski's first feature is an exploration of personal obsessions, not social or political concerns. The tendency to explore the geography of the self
went against the grain of official Marxist aesthetics, with its
stern emphasis on man in society. From the official point of
view, Polanski's solipsistic vision was threatening—even
dangerous—because it coolly denied the imperatives of so-

cialist politics and society. Polanski was not an opposition filmmaker: the censors would know how to deal with that. The tensions among his three characters are erotic, psychological. *Knife in the Water* made one thing clear: Polanski was playing a different game, his own, in isolation from society.

The script carefully places its three characters in a hermetically sealed situation so that they reveal themselves fully to one another—and to the camera. Its action occurs when, confined on a small sailboat amid the brilliant sunlight of an otherwise empty lake, the characters have nowhere to hide. Even a storm doesn't help, forcing them only closer together inside the boat's tiny cabin. The husband, Andrzej, the successful sportswriter, is much devoted to the material possessions his position has earned him. Krystyna, his wife, seems less satisfied with their success, perhaps in part because she too is one of Andrzej's treasured status symbols, a fact suggested by the detail that she and the boat share the same name. The intrusion of the boy inflames the latent tensions between the couple. Young, poor, physically attractive, contemptuous of Andrzej—but also envious—the hitchhiker, whose name no one bothers to ask, is everything the older man is not.

Yet it soon grows apparent that the two men are not so different after all. As Krystyna points out to the boy in a burst of anger: "You are just the same as my husband—or you will be." Instinctively, both men sense the similarity, this awareness pressing them into vicious combat. Each, in turn, finds new ways to humiliate the other as Krystyna—and the camera—watch. Huddled in the damp cabin, all three play a game of forfeits. The loser of each round must forfeit an article of clothing, and since they wear little on board, it will not be long before the players will be entirely naked. In this risk of total exposure, the game mirrors the psychological conflicts and clashes of its players.

As the couple's secret sharer, the hitchhiker is a particularly rich character. If he bears more than just a physical resemblance to Skolimowski, it is because the latter had used some of his own recent anxieties about age and success to flesh out the role. At the beginning, the boy—appropriating a favorite game of Skolimowski's—plays "chicken," jumping in front of Andrzej's oncoming car to force it to stop. Andrzej, who is driving, reacts with fury, fearing that he has been made to look foolish. The ensuing drama is just as threatening to the self-image of the younger man, who treasures the knife he has with him in the way that Andrzej does his car and boat.

Throughout the violence, at first verbal, then physical, between the two men, Krystyna merely observes, teases, provokes—until the end, when suddenly she reveals herself a true master of the tactics of humiliation. The husband, probably by accident, tosses the boy's one treasured possession, the large, nasty knife, overboard. A fight ensues. Much the larger of the two, Andrzej knocks the youth backward onto a sail. Losing his foothold, the boy, who has previously insisted he cannot swim, tumbles into the water and vanishes. Fearing to look foolish, Andrzej first proclaims that the boy is pretending to have drowned. But when the boy doesn't surface, Krystyna jumps into the water, and eventually Andrzej is compelled to follow.

The boy, who *can* in fact swim, is hiding behind a large buoy and cannot be found. Increasingly panicked, the couple must face the probability that he has drowned. Climbing back onto the sailboat, Krystyna begins to scream that Andrzej is a murderer. She taunts him mercilessly with the crime, goading him into swimming to shore to report to the police. As Andrzej disappears from sight, the boy swims back to the boat, where, finally, as he wears Andrzej's bathrobe, he and Krystyna make love—but only after she has told him that he is no better than her husband. Afterward the boy goes ashore, and Krystyna sails in to the dock, where her husband is waiting. Andrzej has not gone to the police, and it is embarrassingly obvious that his claim of having left the car keys on the boat is no more than an excuse.

Krystyna informs her husband of what happened with the boy. In effect, she is offering him a choice between being a murderer, if he believes that the boy has died, or being a cuckold, if he believes that she is telling the truth about the boy's return and her infidelity with him. The film ends with a prolonged shot of the couple sitting in the car again—at a crossroads—unable to turn right or left.

In the film's completed form, both the plot and the visual elements of *Knife in the Water* bear a striking resemblance to those of René Clément's *Purple Noon* (1959), starring Marie Laforêt and Alain Delon. From the central section of Clément's film, Polanski drew inspiration for virtually all the major structural elements of *Knife*. In *Knife* he reworked the psychological dynamics and even pictorial composition of Clément's scrutiny of a couple and a handsome young man in the constricted space of a sailboat. As in *Knife in the Water*, in Clément's film a man's possessions—notably the sailboat and the woman—trigger a dual for power and an exchange of identities. Clément's enigmatic intruder even is associated with a large and menacing knife. On the boat, a game is played that ends in murder. So unavoidable are the parallels between the two films that it is obvious Clément was a director much on Romek's mind when he returned to Poland to rewrite and direct *Knife in the Water*. Moreover, Polanski only recently had enviously eyed Clément's sports car, while waiting for Basia, who was closeted with the French director. It cannot be altogether accidental that the girl Polanski had chosen to play the role of Krystyna—the woman responsible for the humiliation and betrayal of her husband—looked, as Henryk Kluba had noted, distinctly like Romek's own ex-wife.

In addition to receiving a modest payment for the film, Polanski was assured royalties from Polish distribution. Foreign royalties, however, were to go directly to the distributor, Film Polski. In any case, Polanski regarded *Knife in the Water* as his "ticket to the West." After all, making his first feature in Poland had been a second choice. Kosinski felt that Polanski was "too impatient" to go on making films in Poland. Now Polanski could cash in on his ticket —but the authorities would still have their say on any film he made in Poland.

At the Thirteenth Plenary Session of the Communist party, its head, Wladyslaw Gomulka, singled out two films for attack—Wajda's *Innocent Sorcerers* and Polanski's *Knife in the Water*. Gomulka declared that the Polish cinema had no place for such films. Their focus on the personal rather than the social or political rendered them anathema to the Communist party. Polanski was "proud" of being considered important enough to be attacked like this —*and* in the company of a senior artist like Wajda. Suddenly, certain Polish intellectuals who had been contemptuous of Polanski's apolitical attitude began to re-evaluate him, to take him seriously.

But by then he had already made his decision: he was going to Paris again, this time with a completed feature film. Polanski would never defect from Poland, would never give up his Polish passport. Still, Poland could no longer contain his ambitions. More than anything, he wanted to be a commercial director in the West—something he sought to accomplish by moving his base to Paris.

While in Paris, Polanski at last got the big break he had been waiting for—an invitation to the first New York Film Festival, where *Knife in the Water* was to be screened on September 11, 1963. His living conditions in Paris may have been squalid, his clothing threadbare—but Roman Polanski was suddenly on top of the world. In America, *Knife in the Water* had made the cover of *Time* magazine. (From then on, Jerzy Kosinski says, Polanski was called "Time Cover" in Poland, so impressive was his feat.)

New York provided Polanski his first taste of expense-account luxury. The festival put him up at the Americana Hotel, a far cry from his impoverished Parisian quarters. That September, Polanski was just past his thirtieth birthday, but, as usual, people took him for someone much younger. Not yet able to speak English, he talked to the press through translators, at least one of whom was tactful enough to omit his Polish curses and crudities. To the New York *Post*'s Archer Winsten—who called him "cherubic" —Polanski said, "I feel very old. I'm a combination of an old man and a baby." Next, Winsten reported: "He mentioned a man who was afraid to shave for fear he might see an elderly man in the mirror. He mentioned an actor who played young boys for forty years. And suddenly, without having any manhood at all, he played the roles of old men."

Enigmatic at the time, Polanski's anecdote was, of course, an ironic version of his own life. Strangely enough, Winsten's conclusion was equally ironic and knowing: "It is indeed possible that Roman Polanski will be an unnaturally brilliant boy for the next 30 years until suddenly he will be a decrepit boy. Meanwhile, what a life!"

Back in Paris, Polanski was full of his trip to America, his *Time* cover and the marvels of expense accounts. And it was not long before he received yet another invitation to the States. This time *Knife in the Water* had been nominated for an Oscar for the Best Foreign Film of 1963.

In Hollywood—living at the Beverly Hills Hotel—he discovered even greater grandeur than in New York. His guide to the film capital was another Pole, the eminent composer, Academy member and Oscar winner Bronislaw Kaper. For the Hollywood trip, Polanski had acquired an Italian suit, of which he was very proud. As he and Kaper prepared to leave the hotel for the Academy's dinner for foreign nominees, Polanski was so wrought up that he tripped and fell down the hotel stairs, ripping the knee of his trousers. Kaper noted Polanski's anguished look as he rose from his tumble, upset both by his torn trousers and the likelihood that he appeared foolish before his host. But at the party, Polanski soon forgot about his little accident as Kaper squired him about, introducing him to scores of film celebrities. Suddenly Polanski found himself shaking hands with Kaper's friend "King." Kaper watched Polanski's face light up as the legendary Hollywood director King Vidor, after a warm greeting, asked the young director how *he* had managed to light a certain shot in *Knife in the Water*.

five

ONCE *Knife in the Water* was finished, Polanski and Skolimowski knew they couldn't work together again. Skolimowski was beginning his career as a film director, determined not to remain in the subordinate role of screenwriter. Moreover, he had too strong an ego to continue collaborating with Polanski in any capacity. In Paris, Polanski teamed up with a new screenwriter, Gerard Brach. Although at first they weren't able to sell anything, together they wrote scripts for what would become *Repulsion* and *Cul de Sac*.

The lean period ended later in 1963 when the collaborators managed to interest a producer in a project. Polanski was signed to direct one of the episodes in an omnibus film, *The Most Beautiful Swindles in the World,* a sketch called "Amsterdam" or "The Diamond Necklace." The other sections of the omnibus were directed by Jean-Luc Godard, Claude Chabrol and Ugo Gregoretti, so Polanski would be in good company. Polanski's episode details the bizarre adventures of a young woman in Amsterdam who swindles a shop out of a diamond necklace and is then herself swindled out of the prize.

Polanski has said that he got the idea from a story about strange happenings in the world of jewels told by a helpful salesman at Cartier's in Paris. The film was shot on location, in Amsterdam, but Polanski was unable to capture and harness the locale effectively enough to evoke the right atmosphere. The story's pace was slow, the film lacking the tension and ambiguity Polanski usually generated on screen. It was a disappointing first step on a feature film in the West, despite the promise of the nasty joke on which it hinged. It was a Polanskian story, complete with voyeurism, sexual humiliation and a fascination with gratuitous acts, but this time he failed to find the mastery necessary to convey his ideas convincingly.

Soon after "Amsterdam," Polanski met another Polish expatriate, Gene Gutowski, with whom he formed a London-based production company, Cadre Films. Hoping to capitalize on the success of *Knife in the Water*, Polanski needed Gutowski's contacts, business acumen and ability to speak English. In London, Gutowski took Polanski to a meeting with Michael Klinger, the rotund, cigar-chomping head of a small production company, Compton Films, which specialized in soft-core pornography, with titles like *The Yellow Teddy Bears*, *Saturday Night Out* and *Black Torments*. Compton also owned a small chain of cinemas and a very active distribution setup in the United Kingdom. Klinger saw immediately that Polanski was a skilled self-promoter and was drawn to him for that reason. With Polanski, Klinger realized, Compton Films could not only transcend pornography but could make money in the process. Polanski came cheap, and he had experience in an industry that turned out quality products with small budgets—the Polish cinema.

Even before they could really communicate well with each other in English, Klinger began to feel a genuine affection for the boyish director. Polanski and Klinger were soon dining regularly at a Jewish restaurant in Soho owned by an enormous man named "Russian Jack," who was given to insulting customers. Russian Jack had a special trick for those he liked—lowering his big belly onto their table. Whenever Klinger and his little friend came in, Russian Jack would do the trick, to Polanski's delight.

Klinger was amazed as he watched the development of Polanski's English. When he had hardly more than a few words, he was already prepared to trade insults. One day they arrived to find that Russian Jack was away and that his chef, a Greek named George, was insulting guests on behalf of his employer. After a hearty meal and much to drink, Polanski and Klinger lit up cigars. George came over and looked down askance at the Polish director. "You're a bit young to smoke a cigar!" he chided Polanski. Although he was now thirty-one, Polanski looked no more than eighteen. "Well, actually, this is my first cigar," Polanski returned, deadpan. He paused a moment, then continued: "And now I go to have my first woman. Then I come back to fuck you." Whatever the language, however limited in it, Polanski was the same.

Klinger began negotiating with Gutowski and Polanski for a twelve-page outline of a horror feature to be called *Lovely Hatred*. The outline was to be written in French although the film would be British. When Polanski returned to Europe from Los Angeles in May 1964, after the Oscar ceremonies, he and Gutowski went to the south of France for the Cannes Film Festival, where the deal with Compton Films was clinched. But when Brach and Polanski completed their script, and the film was made, it was not a horror work at all but a psychological study called *Repulsion*, a foray into the mind of a schizophrenic. The basis of the story was the illness of a girl Polanski had encountered in Paris. Introverted and taciturn, the girl desired but feared sexual contact.

Repulsion concerns a young Belgian, Carol Ledoux, who lives with her sister in London. Carol's blond, impenetrable beauty hides turbulent sexual chaos beneath the surface, which erupts into murderous violence. Carol's older sister has brought a married lover into the apartment, and their sexual relationship disturbs the girl. The sister and her lover go off on a holiday to Italy, leaving Carol alone. She shuts herself up in the apartment, and gradually, madness overwhelms her. A gentle young Englishman, who has been courting Carol, comes to the flat to see why she has disappeared. Carol imagines that he is there to attack her, and she kills him, battering him with a candlestick, then dumping his body into a full bathtub. Next, violence strikes the sweaty, fat landlord, who mistakes Carol's deepening insanity for seductive languor or physical illness, which would make her vulnerable. The landlord attacks her, and she slashes him brutally with a razor. By the time the sister and her lover return, Carol has killed two men and retreated beneath the sister's bed. The film ends with the sister's boyfriend carrying Carol away from the apartment and the menacing, prying eyes of the neighbors who have come to see the carnage. The film's final image, a view of a snapshot of Carol as a child with her family, suggests that, cuddled in the arms of this older man, she has retreated to a kind of childhood, with both its comforts and its conflicts.

As soon as Polanski and Brach had completed the script, it was adapted, and additional dialogue was added, by David Stone. Casting proved difficult, because of the script's unceasing focus on a single character, Carol. Polanski wanted someone who was at once externally icy and internally demonic—"an angelic-looking girl with a slightly soiled halo," he told *The New York Times*—but no English actress seemed right. It then occurred to him that it might be possible to emphasize the strangeness of the character by casting a foreign actress.

Polanski settled on Catherine Deneuve, a French actress then perhaps best known as another of the creations of that Svengali of the cinema Roger Vadim. A director himself, Vadim had recently fathered her child, without benefit of marriage. Unlike her predecessor with Vadim, Brigitte Bardot, Deneuve had created more of a stir in her off-screen role as Vadim's mistress, flouting social conventions, than in anything she had done on screen.

Polanski was concerned more with Deneuve's natural attributes than with her acting ability, for he was not interested in having Deneuve act her part. Instead, he was bent on having her *experience* Carol's torment. Klinger recalls how Polanski tried to get Deneuve into the proper mood: "He made sure that, in the whole of eight weeks or so when we filmed, Catherine Deneuve didn't get next to a man." Although Polanski could take care of cloistering Deneuve in London, there was the complication that she had just given birth to Vadim's child and wanted to return to Paris to visit the baby. What might happen there was a potential problem. Polanski wanted nothing left to chance, and as financial backer, Klinger was concerned that Deneuve might be detained in Paris, delaying shooting. Polanski did not care at all about money; he only wanted to be certain that his star had no sex during the weeks of the filming.

Ultimately, Klinger began to wear down under Deneuve's pleas for a few days off, until his business sense was overwhelmed. He went to Polanski to discuss letting her go away for the coming weekend. The director agreed to let her go, but he was adamant that it could not be that particular weekend. Klinger was puzzled. What difference did it make when? Polanski explained that he would let Deneuve go the following weekend "because next weekend she'll be having her period. Then I don't mind her going."

Polanski became an adept at generating the proper tension in his actress. The scene in which Carol bashes in the young Englishman's head with a candlestick was shot repeatedly, the crew working late into the afternoon. At the end of the day's shooting, Polanski was particularly unhappy with Deneuve's performance. But he said nothing. The next morning, just after shooting resumed, he provoked her into a fight. The two swore furiously at each other in French. Klinger had never seen Deneuve in such a state. At one point, she tried to control her rage, but Polanski continued to bait her. Then she exploded. He gave her the candlestick and she swung it at him. The camera had been rolling, and now Polanski had the performance he wanted. The Deneuve the spectator sees on screen is not acting—the violence is real, directed at Polanski.

Deneuve was not the only member of the cast whom Polanski treated outrageously. Yvonne Furneaux, another young French actress, had been cast in the role of the older sister. (In 1959 she had played the wife of Marcello Mastroianni in Fellini's *La Dolce Vita*.) A dark-haired, wide-eyed, conscientious professional, Furneaux finally broke down under Polanski's constant badgering. Reduced to tears, she appealed to Klinger to intervene with the director: "He's torturing me. What am I doing wrong? I'm trying so hard." Dismayed, Klinger took Polanski aside. "Why are you giving the girl such a hard time?" he asked. "Michael," Polanski replied, "I know she's a nice girl. She's too bloody nice. She's supposed to be playing a bitch. Every day I have to make her into a bitch."

Tempers of cast and crew were short, for shooting was taking place in the heat of August. As work progressed, it became clear that Polanski had to be given his way—or be made to think that he had. Whenever Klinger attempted to intervene directly, he got nowhere. One particular disagreement concerned an additional murder Polanski and Brach had planned for Carol. In the scene, which ultimately did not find its way into *Repulsion,* the wife of the older sister's lover arrives at the apartment after Carol has claimed her first victim. When the wife discovers the corpse of the young Englishman in the bathtub, Carol drowns her in the bloody water. Klinger found the murder unbelievable in terms of Carol's character, doubting whether she would kill the woman to hide her crime. Polanski responded furiously: Who was Klinger to criticize the psychological accuracy of the script? Polanski was going to shoot the scene and no one was going to stop him. However, when it came time to shoot, the actress he had cast for the part couldn't be persuaded to put her head underwater for the drowning. Too stubborn to give up, Polanski grabbed a mackintosh and blond wig and played the betrayed wife himself in drag.

However, when the jazz musician Chico Hamilton looked at *Repulsion,* in order to conceive its score, he objected to one thing—the murder of the wife. When the lights went on in the screening room, Hamilton turned to Polanski. "There's only one thing wrong with the movie," he said. "What's that woman doing getting killed? That's totally wrong."

Polanski was furious, particularly because Klinger was present. But Klinger, who had opposed the scene from the start, was careful now to say nothing. A day or two later, when Polanski and he were having lunch, the director said casually: "You know, I have an idea. This murder with the woman. It's wrong." "You know," Klinger replied, "you're absolutely right." "You don't mind if I take it out?" asked Polanski. "No," Klinger replied.

Polanski could be expensive if not watched carefully. One of the scenes for *Repulsion* was to be shot on a weekend in the salon of trendy London haircutter Vidal Sassoon, a close friend of Polanski's. Ordinarily, Polanski would shoot a scene only after he had carefully prepared it. But when circumstances forced him to rethink a scene or part of a scene on the spot, he was unwilling to admit any lack of control, even if for a moment. At Sassoon's, Klinger found this out—at great expense. Shooting on Sunday meant triple pay for the crew, so it was important to finish

as quickly as possible. Instead, Polanski became immersed
in a segment of a scene in which the shop's manager picks
up a bottle of nail polish. The hand is viewed in close-up,
the manager remarking, "The wrong color, but the old
bitch will never know." Observing Polanski at work on the
scene, Klinger was puzzled, for the close-up of the hand
could have been an insert shot made anywhere, anytime.
Polanski, he decided, was giving himself time to work
something out. Klinger obligingly stepped out of the shop,
acquiescing to Polanski's expensive tactic to gain himself
time. But when Klinger returned, the director was on his
third take of the close-up—then the fourth, fifth and sixth.
Finally, Klinger exploded: "What the hell is this? We've
got two hundred people here, and you're shooting a hand
and a bottle of nail polish!"

The close-up was shot twenty-seven times, an inexcus-
able waste of money and time. Plotting revenge, Klinger
secretly approached the film's editor, Alistair McIntyre,
whom he thought "a very capable man, but Roman's slave."
"Print the whole lot, all twenty-seven takes," Klinger ordered him, "and don't put the numbers on them. And if
Roman finds out, you're fired." When the rushes were
ready, Klinger invited the unsuspecting Polanski to dinner.
"I have something I want to show you in one of the screening rooms," he said to his guest after dinner. "We're to see
a movie?" Polanski asked. A movie, Klinger agreed, and he
proceeded to screen all twenty-seven takes of the close-up.
After they had seen just a few, Polanski got up to leave.
Klinger barked: "You sit down, you little Polish cock-
sucker! There are twenty-seven of those and you chose
three, and you're gonna tell me which three and why!"

In the end, *Repulsion* pleased everyone involved, and
the tempest of the shooting was quickly forgotten. Klinger
and Compton got the prestige film they wanted. And Polanski had himself a feature that struck a balance between
commercial and artistic success—in short, he had it both
ways, the direction in which his future lay. Reviewing the
film in *Movie*, Peter von Bagh pointed out that Polanski
had "managed to combine the most intellectual cinema
with the most popular."

At first, however, the film encountered censorship problems. The Austrian censors objected immediately. As a result, *Repulsion* was screened for an august group of psychiatrists in Vienna to determine what its effect might be. Afterward, the psychiatrists asked Klinger where Polanski had studied psychiatry. They not only approved the film, but described Carol Ledoux as a perfect textbook case of schizophrenia.

Polanski now had been given the seal of seriousness. *Repulsion* was no cheap exploitation film but a valid study of sexual madness. A British psychiatrist who had looked at the script had deemed Polanski "perfectly balanced" because of his obvious comprehension of madness. Polanski, who, by his own account, had always taken himself "for a madman," was upset at being lumped in with such "balanced people" as bankers, grocers and others "with good intentions."

Repulsion was entered in the Berlin Film Festival, where it won a Silver Bear, the second-highest award. Cannes turned down *Repulsion,* but Klinger was too smart to miss out on this biggest of all film markets. He took both film and director to the south of France, where he screened it himself. Polanski was a sensation. He worked the festival brilliantly, mixing arrogance, insult and boyish charm. Even at that early stage of his career, *Repulsion* was explicitly billed as "Roman Polanski's"—the director's name above the title. The little-known filmmaker was being sold as much as his film.

Repulsion was Polanski's first Western feature, but its theme and technique were fully consistent with the audacity of his earlier work. The first image—an enormous eye, which fills the screen—suggests that, once again, Polanski is obsessed with the world of the voyeur. *Repulsion* involves a foray into the subjectivity of Carol Ledoux, whose eye this is. In the film's closing shot, the camera moves closer and closer toward *another* eye, that of Carol as a child, registered in an old photograph. This last shot oddly parallels the first, as the child's eye fills the screen.

This key repetition suggests that, for Polanski, madness —specifically of the sexual sort chronicled in the film—has its origin in childhood. Significantly, the child's eye is shown in the context of the family romance, the idyllic relations, real or imagined, of child and parents. In this final shot, a shadow casts a distinct triangular grid over the photograph, thereby linking father, mother and child. The father clearly is the object of Carol's gaze, revealing the source of her relationship with her sister's lover.

A Belgian living in London, Carol is an outsider, an on-looker—a situation that is duplicated by her situation with her mock family. When not otherwise preoccupied, her older sister behaves with Carol like an indulgent mother. The sister and her lover have a tendency to toy with Carol, to make promises of shared family dinners and then forget them. That the rabbit on a sideboard is left to rot is signifi-cant, for Carol's suitor calls her "Poor Bunny," thereby linking her to the decaying, abandoned beast. Just as the sister and her lover leave the rabbit behind, so they aban-don "Poor Bunny." She is the third party, the unwanted extra.

Spying on the love affair, Carol is the voyeuristic child-witness of furtive embraces, the nocturnal listener to the sounds of lovemaking. Lying in her narrow bed on the other side of the wall, she seems doomed to an endless childhood, from which she escapes only in her fantasies. These fantasies involve violence, which eventually spills over into reality when she feels most abandoned. *Repul-sion* is Polanski's chronicle of childish feelings of rejection and expulsion, ones he knew well from personal experi-ence. The child's view that the sexual act is a violent one is reflected in Carol's repeated fantasy of anal rape by a blurry male figure, who appears from nowhere.

Polanski evinces an uncanny comprehension of this fe-male character and her tormented, childish vision. His probing scrutiny of her is a kind of voyeurism, a violation of her most private moments. It is remarkable how little significant dialogue there is in *Repulsion*, in which a state of mind is conveyed *cinematically*, through the merciless inspection of Carol's face and gestures for what they reveal. Years later, in *The Tenant*, the director would himself per-form an ironic version of Carol, in drag, suggesting his fas-cination—even identification—with the "Carol" character. *The Tenant* would make explicit what could only be guessed at in *Repulsion*—the voyeur's projection of exhibitionistic impulses into the object of his gaze. In *Repulsion*—as, later, in *Tess*—Polanski projects himself into the vulnerable female victim as he subjects her to the camera's stare.

Some reviewers were disturbed by the clinical bent of *Repulsion*. *The Christian Science Monitor* called it a study of "morbid psychology" and complained that "for all its technical accomplishment, after seeing *Repulsion*, one leaves the cinema feeling bruised and soiled." Peter John Dyer, in *Sight and Sound*, speculated that *Repulsion* "hardly seems designed to cater for the taste of anyone other than a trained psychiatrist. . . . Its possible effect on anybody going through a period of crisis or depression doesn't bear thinking about."

In an interview with *Lettres Françaises*, Polanski insisted that he hadn't made a Freudian film. The childhood sources of Carol's madness, he said, did not interest him. He sought merely to describe Carol, not probe her motivations. Still, despite his claims, Polanski had left clues leading to Carol's childhood—and his. As in a dream, two of Romek's key images of violence—a blow to the head; blood mingling with water—turn up in *Repulsion*, but in a displaced form, so that it is Carol, his avatar, who causes them: the victim turned victimizer. The baring and denial of the psychological sources of his material—in Carol and himself—is the sort of contradiction that is typical of Polanski.

In the film's final sequence, Romek the prankster undercuts Polanski the serious filmmaker when the apartment where Carol has wrought such havoc is invaded by grotesque and nosy neighbors. "One of them," wrote the critic Dwight Macdonald, "an aged man in a bathrobe, totters into the living room, sees the feet of the . . . corpse, and totters out, registering shock so violently the scene got a laugh that could not have been the director's intention." Not Polanski's intention but *Romek's*. What Macdonald could not have known when he wrote his critique in 1966 was that, both as filmmaker and man, Polanski would constantly be plagued by contradictory impulses, an unsettling tendency to submit even the most poignant and personal events to scathing and subversive laughter.

In his next film, *Cul de Sac*, Polanski again created a

deeply personal work, a commercial feature shot through with autobiographical significance. The success of *Repulsion* had put him in a position to ask almost anything he wanted of Compton. So he offered a script he had written with Brach in Paris in 1963, a work originally called *When Kattelbach Comes*. The script eventually became the absurdist masterpiece *Cul de Sac*.

Among certain of Polanski's Polish friends, it is understood that *Cul de Sac* was written in homage to Basia Kwiatkowska. By 1965 it was four years since she had left him, but Polanski's desire to make *Cul de Sac* indicated that he had not forgotten her. The starring female role, in fact, was first offered to Kwiatkowska herself. Polanski agreed to search for another actress only when Basia's husband refused to allow her to accept the part. *Cul de Sac*, then, is Polanski's fictionalized portrait of his marriage to Basia, his humiliation by her, and his continued longing. Not only did he originally plan for Basia to play the female lead, he intended to play her humiliated transvestite husband. When Klinger rejected the idea of Polanski's working both sides of the camera, Françoise Dorléac and Donald Pleasence were cast.

Cul de Sac is the story of a middle-aged Englishman living in shabby splendor with his second wife, a Frenchwoman much younger than he, in an isolated island castle. The highly sexual wife alternately ignores and taunts her husband. After cuckolding him on the beach with the slim, blond son of some visiting neighbors (a role played by Iain Quarrier, an actor who bore a marked resemblance to Polanski's own nemesis, Basia's husband, Karl Heinz Boehm), she flaunts her rejection of him. At other times, as when she persuades him to dress in one of her frothy nightgowns, her makeup smeared on his face, her humiliating tactics seem almost affectionate. Blind to her abuse, or pretending to be, the husband is an absurd but touching figure.

Into the perverse isolation of husband and wife wanders a pair of intruders, two wounded criminals. One of them, played by Jack MacGowran, dies shortly after their arrival; the other, his slightly wounded companion, played by Lionel Stander, embarks on a mercurial and bizarre relationship with the couple. He holds them in a grotesque period of captivity while waiting to be rescued by the boss of the gang he belonged to. Strange shifting alliances and power games develop among husband, wife and gangster. In the end, to his own amazement, the husband shoots the intruder. Just then his wife abandons him, taking off across the beach as the rising tide cuts off the island's access to the mainland. The tormented husband is left perched atop a rock, surrounded by water, crying out over and over the name of his first wife.

In the initial planning, the first thing Klinger wanted resolved was the question of Gutowski's role in the production of *Cul de Sac*. Klinger feared that Gutowski would act as a buffer for Polanski in his relations with Compton. On *Repulsion*, Klinger felt, Gutowski had operated as producer in name only, leaving most of the day-to-day problems to Klinger. When, in private, with Polanski, Klinger broached the subject of Gutowski's role, the director balked at the idea of cutting his partner. Klinger realized that as admirable as Polanski's loyalty to his partner might seem, it was not spurred by altruism alone. Klinger felt that "Roman always needs a doormat." Nor was Gutowski the only pal Polanski wanted. He informed Klinger that another expatriate Polish crony must be brought in on the project as well, Sam Waynberg, then living in Germany. Thus, the production of *Cul de Sac* was set up with Polanski directing, Gutowski and Waynberg producing, and Klinger's company again backing what would be a difficult and troubled project.

The budget was slightly larger than the one for *Repulsion*, but at the £135,000 alotted was certainly, even then, a modest sum. Waynberg, who put up some of the money, suggested the film be shot in Yugoslavia. But Polanski, having just left Poland, wanted no part of filming in Eastern Europe, although he did agree to make a trip to Yugoslavia to scout for locations. The trip, of course, proved to be abortive. Then, as he had intended all along, he hired a plane and flew up the English coast, until, off Northumberland, he found Holy Island, a barren rock cut off from the mainland twice a day by the tide.

Shooting was difficult. The weather was brutal—cold and unusually rainy. Cast and crew were housed in the cottages of the island's few inhabitants—mostly salmon fishermen—and the forced close contact intensified the conflicts that arose from the shooting.

Donald Pleasence created a stir the moment he descended on the island, with its two tiny roads and humble inhabitants, for he drove a mammoth and opulent Lincoln the likes of which Holy Island had never seen. Moreover, the first day of shooting, Pleasence arrived on the set with his head shaved. Even Polanski was taken aback: "It's not a good idea, old boy," he mumbled.

Françoise Dorléac had been selected to play the role of the wife on the advice of her sister, Catherine Deneuve, after Polanski had interviewed more than two hundred English actresses, none of whom satisfied him. The two sisters could not have played more different characters for Polanski. While Deneuve's Carol was sexually repressed, Dorléac's Teresa was a nymphomaniac, her girlish innocence shot through with sensuality. The husband calls his wife "baby" and "my little girl," and one of the criminals alludes to the castle as a place for orgies with little girls. This Polanski "little girl" is a highly sexual being, hardly an innocent at all, but given to teasing, even to humiliating, her adoring husband. Taken together, *Repulsion* and *Cul de Sac* offer an odd view of women, either sexually repressed and mad or nymphomaniacal and castrative. As unfaithful bitch, the wife in *Cul de Sac* echoes the wife in *Knife in the Water*.

Polanski's relations with the twenty-three-year-old Dorléac were tempestuous. Determined to play the role of the movie star, Dorléac arrived on the island with seventeen suitcases and a lapdog named Jaderane. The vicious dog soon became Polanski's bête noire, because Dorléac would go nowhere without it. Polanski was stymied until helped by an act of God. Dorléac chipped a tooth early in shooting and flew to a dentist in France, taking Jaderane. When, during her return, she attempted to conceal the dog from English customs by stuffing it in her bag, Jaderane bit the customs officer's hand and was confiscated.

Dorléac, however, had grievances of her own. She felt that Polanski's treatment of her was manipulative, as if she were an object. Although she was eventually satisfied with

the film, she complained bitterly about Polanski's problems
in communicating with women.

At one point, Dorléac was caught in the middle of a
power game Polanski and Klinger were playing. Klinger
had been appalled at the slow pace of the production.
When he then lamented that Polanski was shooting only
half a page of script a day, Polanski grabbed the script from
him and started to flip pages—fourteen of them—boasting
that he could shoot all in a single day. To do it, Polanski
worked Dorléac's body nearly beyond human limits. The
scene that resulted, a single long take, is one of the longest
shots in cinematic history. It also nearly brought the production of *Cul de Sac* to a halt.

The notorious scene depicts a row between Stander and
Pleasence. The husband is motivated, in much of this, by
torment over his wife's infidelity. Dorléac appears from the
castle, undresses and slips into the water. Meanwhile, on
the beach the drunken row continues, until an airplane is
spotted. The gangster thinks the plane has come to pick
him up and fires a revolver at it, to catch its attention. But
the plane disappears. Dorléac emerges from the water and
goes back to the castle, and the original drunken row continues as before. In a single long take, the camera can't stop
running. Therefore, although Dorléac couldn't be seen
while she was in the icy water, she had to remain there
until it was time to come out.

When Polanski ordered shooting to begin, Dorléac did as
she was told, entering the water stark naked and remaining
until it was time for her to reappear in the shot. When she
emerged, her body was blue from the cold. Without a
pause, Polanski barked, "We go again!" Klinger couldn't
believe that the director was going to retake the shot without giving Dorléac a break. Besides, the first take had
worked. But the shot was set up for a second time. Once
again the take was perfect, with seven or eight minutes of
brilliant acting, and Polanski had two takes in the can.

By now, Dorléac had darkened from blue to purple.
Klinger complained that she was half-frozen. The director
seemed unconcerned. He wasn't certain he had what he
needed. "We're going again!" he said. The shot was set up
for a third time. Dorléac stripped off her robe, and plunged

into the water and collapsed. Crew members rushed in to save her. She began to menstruate, and the company doctor feared that she might have suffered a minor heart attack. The set exploded into pandemonium. The usually aloof British crew had reached its limit. The shop steward announced that the crew would go on strike if Polanski continued his mistreatment of the actress. At last he had to back down.

Dorléac experienced more abuse during the shooting of one of the film's funniest scenes, in which she is paired with Stander. The gangster has fallen asleep, and Dorléac sneaks up and gives him a hotfoot, lighting a piece of paper inserted between his toes. Awakening enraged, the gangster knocks the woman to the ground, throws himself upon her, and whips her with a belt. Pinned, chestdown, to the cobblestones, Dorléac flinched in pain, causing Stander to yell, "You bitch, you hurt me! You moved!" Polanski was having difficulty getting the scene precisely as desired, and it was shot several times, Dorléac experiencing the full force of Stander's strength as he would throw her to the ground and whip her with his belt. The exhausted actress complained to Polanski, but to no avail. Again and again the brutal scene was repeated until the director was satisfied.

If Dorléac bent under Polanski's tough regimen, Stander was more the director's match. One day, cast and crew were eating lunch, when Polanski turned to Stander, began to ask him a question, then hesitated. The curious Stander asked what Polanski wanted, "Well," Polanski said, "could you drink a pint of milk in one go?" The gargantuan actor scornfully replied, "Sure!" Pretending to be impressed, but still dubious, Polanski continued, "You can?" Stander rose to the challenge. "Certainly. I'll try it." With this, Stander grabbed a full bottle of milk and downed it without a pause. When he finished, Polanski looked at his watch, "Fantastic. Eleven seconds. Can you do that when we shoot?" "Sure," Stander replied. Sixteen takes were required—sixteen pints of milk—to get the scene done to Polanski's satisfaction. For another scene, Polanski had Stander's gangster eat twenty-two raw eggs.

But Stander's most grueling feat was performed for the

scene in which he buries the other gangster. Stander has to take the body, which is lying on the table, wrap it up, and carry it to the grave. The catch is that he has to do it with one hand—the other arm being useless in a sling. Although MacGowran was small, it was decided that the scene had better be shot with the elfin Gerard Brach doubling for him to make the job easier for Stander. But even Brach became too heavy as Polanski required his usual series of retakes. Finally, Stander managed to haul the body as far as the grave and toss it to Donald Pleasence, who was digging below. In the process, Stander suffered a slight hernia. Later, when he and Polanski looked at the rushes for the scene, Stander was justly chagrined: because of the way the shot was framed, all that could be seen on the screen were his feet. He turned to Polanski and said gruffly, "I don't mind getting a hernia, but I'd like the audience to see me getting it."

Later, Polanski's temper got the best of him, and he nearly lost control of his film. Klinger had descended on the island to look at rushes, and he began the screening without Polanski, who was twenty minutes late for their appointment. Actually, Polanski was hiding behind some curtains, to see if Klinger would start without him. Outraged by the event, Polanski shouted, "Never in all my experience have I been treated like this!" "What experience?" Klinger shot back. "You've made three films in your whole life, and two of them have been for me!" Polanski then yelled, "I quit!" "Good!" Klinger snapped. "Piss off! And remember, there's a director in London waiting to come out and finish this film, and you'd better pray he's good 'cause when it goes out, it's gonna say, 'Directed by Roman Polanski.' " Polanski stormed out and took off in his Mini. When he returned, an emissary was dispatched to Klinger. "Roman says that he'll stay—if you apologize," the emissary reported. Klinger somehow knew that Polanski was in the vicinity, listening. "Is he still here?" Klinger shouted. "Kick him off the island!" But Klinger, the businessman, had been kidding, only having some fun at his artist's expense.

Cul de Sac was decidedly a Roman Polanski film. Its obsessional tone, its fascination with the mechanics of power and humiliation, its claustrophobic world—these are as definitive Polanski trademarks as are violence and voyeurism. Jean de Baroncelli wrote in *Le Monde* that what strikes the viewer in *Cul de Sac* is the *auteur*'s personality, the coherence of his cinematic universe. In *Humanité*, Samuel Lachize remarked on Polanski's personal vision as expressed in his films. Already, with only his third feature film, Polanski had established a style. The film's eccentric vision aroused speculation about the director. Precisely whose was the claustrophobic world of *Cul de Sac*, people wondered.

Aware of the curiosity the film generated, Romek, in public, began to overplay the brash young artist, or as Jerzy Kosinski described him, "the socialist brat." The Polish critic Krzysztof Toeplitz, who saw *Cul de Sac* at Cannes, where it was privately screened, remarked on how Polanski manipulated the moguls there with his insults and quips. Another of Polanski's Polish friends felt that Romek had paid an enormous price in "playing the Polish clown" to the amused movie crowd. There was something "pathetic and humiliating" in Romek's new role, in his struggle for attention in the West, the friend thought.

One of Polanski's most notorious public relations coups, however, was carried off on behalf of another Polish director, his collaborator on *Knife in the Water*, Skolimowski, who was in Cannes with a new picture of his own. In Poland, Skolimowski was already a well-known filmmaker, an object of great public curiosity and speculation; but in Cannes, he was just another director, if a startlingly handsome one. A press conference for Skolimowski had been called, but it was unlikely to attract much attention. So Polanski, with his knack for obtaining publicity, conceived a strategy for helping his Polish friend. Louis Marcorelles, the French film critic, had just begun to introduce Skolimowski to the press, when Polanski noisily arrived with some friends. Jumping up to the microphone, Polanski abruptly cut in, stopping the perplexed Marcorelles in midsentence: "I know Skolimowski better!" insisted Polanski. "He's a friend of mine. And if you don't mind, *I* will introduce the film." Stunned, Marcorelles had no alternative but to step aside. Polanski looked at the audience of writers and journalists and said, "Skolimowski's a friend of mine, and there is some gossip about him, that he is a homosexual. Believe me, he is not."

With these words, Polanski walked off, having just made his friend an instant celebrity at Cannes. After the film, hordes of the curious at the festival turned out to catch a glimpse of the dashing young director. Polanski's daring hint of scandal had been enough to gain Skolimowski the interest his work deserved.

six

WHILE MAKING *Repulsion* and *Cul de Sac*, Polanski became
a fixture of the swinging London scene. The Italian director
Michelangelo Antonioni gave the period its symbol in
Blow-Up, a film about a voyeuristic fashion photographer
who makes love to women with his ever present camera.
Antonioni best captured the openness—and aimlessness—
of London's cool world, its kaleidoscope of fashion, sex and
sensation. This was the world Polanski inhabited. His base
was London's Playboy Club, whose director at that time
was the urbane Victor Lownes. Lownes, who had been dispatched to London by Hugh Hefner to open the English
branch of Playboy's international operation, was drawn to
what he termed Polanski's "electricity and charisma," and
he soon became the director's closest friend. He offered
Polanski an easy access to beautiful women.

Over drinks and dinner at the Playboy Club—as the bunnies and other beauties looked on—Polanski would tell
jokes in mangled English, duly corrected by Lownes. It
was during these madcap kibitzing sessions that Polanski
began painlessly to master his adopted language. The two
were an odd sight at the dinner table each evening—the
huge, gangly figure of Lownes towering over the diminutive director. Because of a slight facial resemblance, they
were often mistaken for father and son, or older and
younger brother.

"At that time I was really swinging," Polanski recalled.
"All I was interested in was to fuck a girl and move on."
Much of his womanizing was in the company of Lownes,
with whom he often shared girls. This led to fierce competition between them—and heated arguments. As one male
friend perceived, Lownes and Polanski "wanted to fuck the
maximum number of girls." Besides promoting sex, the
Playboy philosophy values male camaraderie. The actress

Barbara Parkins found it impossible to break in when Polanski and Lownes were talking. For her "it was the kind
of relationship where women get terribly jealous, because
it was a love that a woman can't have with a man. . . . Two
men can have it. It's not necessarily sexual. It can be physical. It's a closeness that no woman can penetrate. Women
used to go crazy because they'd want to get Roman or Victor's attention, and it couldn't be done."

With Lownes, Polanski discovered and learned to enjoy
the accouterments of the good life Playboy-style—fine food
and drink, hi-fis, sports cars, and especially the women.
Back in Poland, Polanski's first feature had been about the
seductiveness of possessions—and the attendant danger.
Now, in mod London, he became attuned to the Playboy
life and its pleasures and privileges. Across the Atlantic in
the States, *Playboy* magazine ran an item on the club's new
recruit, introducing readers to "Bolshevism's boy wonder"
as someone to watch. Even today a portrait of Polanski—an
oil painting by Leroy Nieman—hangs in the VIP Room of
the London Playboy Club.

The *Playboy* item ran in the October 1966 issue, accompanied by a still from Polanski's latest film, *The Fearless
Vampire Killers*, billed as a "horror spoof." The issue also
pictured the director, sporting breeches and a waist-length
jacket in the film's leading role.

After *Repulsion* and *Cul de Sac*, Polanski's strategy had
been to obtain Hollywood money for *The Fearless Vampire
Killers*. The producer Martin Ransohoff, of Filmways,
agreed to finance the picture for Cadre, the Polanski-Gu-
towski company, with a budget of $1.7 million, vast in com-
parison with Polanski's earlier budgets. But Ransohoff
exacted a big concession: if he was not satisfied with the
completed film, he could re-edit it for America. Polanski
wanted Hollywood financing badly enough to agree to Ransohoff's terms.

Ransohoff suggested his protégée Sharon Tate for the
film's lead. The producer had met her four years earlier
when she auditioned for TV's "Petticoat Junction." He had
signed the buxom nineteen-year-old beauty to an exclusive
seven-year contract but had kept her under wraps. "Mr.
Ransohoff didn't want the audience to see me till I was

ready," Tate told *Playboy*. (When she appeared on TV—in "Petticoat Junction," "The Beverly Hillbillies," and "Mr. Ed"—it was under an assumed name and often in a black wig.)

At the time Polanski was preparing to shoot *The Fearless Vampire Killers*, Sharon was in London playing a sorceress in a movie about witchcraft and ritual sacrifice, *Eye of the Devil*. Back in the States, she had been romantically involved with tiny, boyish-looking Jay Sebring, who was known as "hairdresser to the stars" because of his popularity among Hollywood celebrities. Sebring was a friend of Victor Lownes, and when Sharon came to London, he asked Lownes to "look after her." Ransohoff had shown Polanski Sharon's photos, but although the director was impressed by her looks, he did not want anyone to tell him whom to hire for a major part. He later met Sharon for the first time at a party at Lownes's house but still was not especially struck by her. Nevertheless, he deferred to Ransohoff and gave her a screen test—in which he saw something he had not seen before. He cast her at once.

Sharon was to play Sarah, a delectable and naive girl menaced by stalking vampires. Opposite her, Polanski himself was cast as Sarah's bumbling protector, the laughably lovesick student Alfred, the fellow in the breeches pictured in *Playboy*. Deciding that many actors would find the role humiliating, and that it suited him quite perfectly, Polanski had chosen to play Alfred, his first major role in a film of his own.

Polanski arranged to shoot *The Fearless Vampire Killers* at a chateau in the Italian Alps. Most exteriors were filmed on location in the Dolomites, near Ortisei. The production company overwhelmed the secluded village with the massive equipment they brought in. But the locals were most amazed by the cargo in the production caravan: 20 gallons of imitation blood, 50 gallons of imitation port wine and 18,000 garlic bulbs—while the six-fanged dental plates probably escaped notice. The imitation blood was a special Polanski recipe, the ingredients of which he refused to reveal. The imitation port wine was for a vampires' ball. (Polanski, who would require numerous takes for each scene, didn't want his cast drunk.) Garlic bulbs were traditional for warding off vampires. In addition, Polanski brought two wolves from the Rome zoo. Local carpenters were commissioned to make the dozens of coffins needed.

That year the snows melted early, forcing Polanski to complete shooting at the MGM studios near London. Back in England, a mock chateau was constructed, the desired snow simulated with forty tons of a salt and polystyrene mixture.

Written with Gerard Brach, *The Fearless Vampire Killers* again makes extensive use of the voyeuristic impulse. When Alfred and his mentor, the "fearless vampire killer" Professor Abronsius—played by Jack MacGowran—take a room at a rural inn, the student is drawn to a keyhole disclosing an adjoining bathroom. Peering into the keyhole, Alfred sees Sarah bathing in a tub, her voluptuous flesh clothed only in suds. (The scene recalls Polanski's 1957 student short *Toothy Smile*, in which a beauty in her bath is spied on by a Peeping Tom.) Presently Sarah's father— played by Alfie Bass—enters the bathroom and spanks her, punishment for her obsessive washing, a clearly sense-gratifying habit she has picked up at school. Alfred is delighted. In spite of Sarah's voluptuousness, she is still a child—as witnessed by her soft, girlish voice and finger in her mouth—a child who can be turned over Daddy's knee for a spanking.

Excited by his furtive vision of pleasure and punishment, Alfred energetically builds his little girl a snowman in front of the inn while she watches from her window. (Her appearance at the window echoes a similar shot of Basia Kwiatkowska in Polanski's Lodz graduation film, *When Angels Fall.*) Alfred's caprice is shattered by snowballs thrown by passing children. Embarrassed, he slips into the inn, where, by way of compensation, he impishly tries to fondle a serving maid's breasts.

The perverse implications of voyeurism are underscored in a scene in which Sarah comes to Alfred's room asking to take a forbidden bath in his tub. Delighted to help, Alfred carefully draws the hot water for her, then steps outside to observe through the keyhole. Thereafter, Count von Krolock, the vampire—played by Ferdy Mayne—who has been secretly spying on Sarah from a window above, swoops down and ravishes her in the tub, while Alfred watches through the keyhole, helplessly paralyzed by fear.

Polanski's *The Fearless Vampire Killers* is a parody of the horror genre, exposing its submerged content, much hinted at but formerly rarely overt on screen. Interestingly, the undercurrent of homosexuality that pervades most conventional vampire movies surfaces quite clearly in Polanski's spoof. Herbert, the count's effeminate son—played by Iain Quarrier, who had become a close friend of Polanski's —focuses his homoerotic desires on young Alfred. Von Krolock has taken Sarah away to his castle, and Alfred pursues them there. He hears Sarah's voice and enters a room, to discover her singing and scrubbing herself in a bathtub. Later, he hears her song again, and he again hastens to her bathroom but finds the bleached-blond Herbert, wearing only a ruffled white shirt, filling the tub. This scene also recalls *Toothy Smile*, in which the voyeur, hoping once more to glimpse the bathing woman, finds a man instead.

Herbert, who is much the larger, now suggests that Alfred is pale and ought to lie down. Stuttering, Alfred allows himself to be lured to tne bed, where Herbert remarks on his "thumpity, thumpity little heart." Alfred is carrying a volume from the castle's library—a manual of one hundred ways of avowing one's love—and Herbert randomly selects the seventieth method, putting his arm around the student's shoulders. Next, Herbert compares his bedmate's eyelashes to "golden threads," when Alfred notices that only he is reflected in the mirror opposite, confirming that Herbert, like his father, is a vampire. Still following the manual, Herbert is about to "brush the lips of the young lady"—actually to suck the young man's blood with his fangs—when Alfred snatches the book and slams it into the vampire's fangs. Thus Polanski establishes the link between vampirism and homosexual love-play that underlies less explicit encounters in the genre.

However, heterosexual desire is at the heart of the film —and its single object is Sharon Tate. During shooting, Polanski had become Sharon's lover. As he recalled later: "When we were on location shooting the film, I asked her, 'Would you like to make love to me?' and she said, very sweetly, 'Yes.' And then for the first time I was somewhat touched by her, you know. And we started sleeping regularly together. And she was so sweet and so lovely that I didn't believe it, you know. I'd had bad experiences and I didn't believe that people like that existed, and I was waiting a long time for her to show the color, right? But she was *beautiful*, without this phoniness. She was fantastic. She loved me."

Polanski declared his feelings in the film's opening credits, when a drop of bright red blood drips down the screen from name to name until, upon reaching Sharon's, it assumes the shape of a heart. In the film, Polanski emphasizes Sarah's essential childishness and passivity—traits that drew him to Sharon. When Jerzy Kosinski first met Sharon Tate he thought she was fourteen and didn't talk to her: "She didn't mind it either. She didn't expect anyone to talk to her." Kosinski was astonished when Polanski revealed that Sharon was no teenager.

When the film was completed, Polanski made the glossy pages of *Playboy* again, but this time he was *behind* the camera, the photographer of six stills, labeled "The Tate Gallery," shot during the filming. The first photo shows Sharon draped with a shabby blue towel but otherwise naked, her breasts and buttocks exposed. In the second image, her eyes are not even visible, just the dropped lids, mascara and false eyelashes; the lower portion of her body and her hands are concealed beneath the suds. "I adore it," says Sarah, in the film. "I got into the habit at school." Using the woman he loved, Polanski staged one of the most private of moments and offered it for the titillation of countless men—surely an ultimate violation.

Soft-core images in a magazine like *Playboy* generally exclude an explicit male presence. But on the next two pages, Count von Krolock hovers over Sharon's body, which drips with suds. "Like us," the blurb announces, von Krolock "finds Sharon a very tasty dish, indeed." Throughout, the director's instructions are only implicit in the slightly licentious poses. Sharon's complicity is evident, her willingness to expose herself for the director, who is, by now, also her lover. Shortly after completing *The Fearless Vampire Killers*, Sharon moved into Polanski's London mews house. And about this time, she was able to purchase her way out of her seven-year contract with Ransohoff.

When Ransohoff screened *The Fearless Vampire Killers,* he was disappointed and exercised his right to final cut, re-editing and redubbing for American release. (Not until the eighties was it rereleased in America in its original form.) Hysterical, Polanski demanded that his name be removed from the bastard version, but Filmways calmly reminded him of his contractual obligations, and his directing credit stayed. Despite warnings that Hollywood money could bury an obnoxious director, Polanski took to the press. Calling Ransohoff a pig and a hypocrite, Polanski claimed that he had been seduced into signing away the final cut. Predicting correctly that Ransohoff's changes would prove disastrous and that *Vampire Killers* therefore would flop in the States, Polanski realized it was essential to acquire a new Hollywood project before the butchered film was released.

seven

AFTER ALFRED HITCHCOCK turned down the film rights to *Rosemary's Baby*, William Castle bought them for $150,000 —three weeks before publication of the novel—hoping to direct the picture himself. Castle had produced and directed grade-B horror films, but now he wanted something better. Reading Ira Levin's thriller, he knew that this was it. Then under contract to Paramount, Castle took the galleys to Robert Evans, the new vice president in charge of production. Evans, who admired Castle's business sense, read it and liked it, but disagreed on one thing: Castle, he felt, wasn't right to direct. Castle made exploitation films and was good at it, but this project needed someone artistic *and* commercial. Suddenly Evans thought of Roman Polanski. Before becoming head of production in Hollywood, Evans had directed Paramount's European production team in London, where he had seen and admired *Repulsion*.

Roman Polanski was a natural for Hollywood. His interests were right—perverse sex, violence, madness, the bizarre—and he was a skilled technician, someone who could take a camera apart and put it together again. Most important, he wasn't a pointy-head director, making high-art for the select few. He had little patience with the arcane or elliptical. In short, he was an arty filmmaker for the mass market—perfect for *Rosemary's Baby*.

Charles Bluhdorn, chairman of the board of Gulf and Western—Paramount's owners—called Castle in and offered to let him produce. Castle would get $250,000 and 50 percent of the profits. But Castle wanted something more —to direct. Bluhdorn suggested that Castle meet Polanski; only then could he judge. Reluctantly, Castle agreed. Evans meanwhile was smart enough to know that Polanski was ambitious and wanted Hollywood and commercial success. But he guessed that, having directed *Repulsion* and *The Fearless Vampire Killers*, Polanski might be leery of being typed as a horror director. Evans decided to lure him to Hollywood with other bait and count on his falling for *Rosemary's Baby* once he got to town. Polanski was an avid skier, and Evans knew it, so when he contacted Polanski in London he invited him to fly over to discuss *Downhill Racer*, based on a novel about a skier, for Paramount.

As soon as Polanski arrived, Evans gave him *Racer* to read that night. Then, almost as an afterthought, he pulled out the galleys of *Rosemary's Baby*. Polanski might want to look at them too. When Evans saw Polanski the next day, he asked him about *Downhill Racer*. Polanski said he wanted to make *Rosemary's Baby*.

Polanski had seen something irresistible in Levin's book —himself. Although Levin later denied it, Polanski thought the novelist must have seen *Repulsion* and been influenced by it. How otherwise account for his own feeling of familiarity?

For a strong director like Polanski—with a vision all his own—a story by someone else can serve as a pretext for a highly personal film, shot through with the director's spirit. This was what happened with *Rosemary's Baby*. When Evans asked who would write the screenplay, Polanski replied that he would. Evans worried about Polanski's still imperfect English. After all, this was a multimillion-dollar project. But Polanski insisted he had to do it himself. He promised Evans that if it didn't work out, he would allow Paramount to bring in someone else. Deciding to gamble, Evans agreed.

But first Polanski had to get Castle's approval. Still eager to direct the film himself and now resentful of Polanski, Castle was prepared to dislike him and at first he did. When they met in Castle's office, the cigar-chomping fifty-three-year-old director-producer sneered at Polanski's mod clothes and his tendency to watch himself in the mirror. But when they talked about *Rosemary's Baby*, Polanski won Castle over. Castle called Paramount and gave his approval. Polanski flew back to London to write the script.

Meanwhile, the William Morris Agency negotiated Polanski's contract with Paramount. There wasn't much to bargain about. Polanski, Paramount felt, was lucky to get the chance to work in Hollywood. He was offered a flat fee of $150,000 to write and direct—and nothing from the net proceeds of the film. At the time the contract was signed, no one imagined that the picture would gross more than $30 million. In any case, Polanski had little choice but to accept Paramount's terms.

Three weeks of seclusion produced a 260-page first draft, with dialogue lifted directly from the novel. Back in the States, Polanski rented a house in Malibu—selected by Castle—and teamed up with Richard Sylbert, his art director for *Rosemary's Baby*, to rewrite. Sylbert helped Polanski scour the script, although he received no screenwriting credit. Sylbert and Polanski acted all the roles, permitting them to fine-tune the characters. Within a month, they had trimmed the first draft by 100 pages. In adaptation, *Rosemary's Baby* was Polanski's own.

At Paramount, Polanski spent hours with an artist, describing his image of characters—physiognomy, build, clothing. It was like detailing a criminal's looks for a composite drawing at police headquarters. Assistant Producer Dona Holloway was amazed at his precise sense of each character. Polanski knew exactly what he wanted and kept the artist working until the image was right. A finished sketch was then completed, and Paramount's production team found the actors who fitted Polanski's needs. There was no question about it: Roman Polanski was virtually in total control, a European-style *auteur* who insisted on getting his conception on screen. For Polanski, a film had to be "the vision of a single person"—despite the numerous collaborators involved, the big budget, the studio bureaucracy. Working in Hollywood, Polanski became acutely aware of the myriad obstacles that stood between his concept and the rushes.

Gradually, with utmost care, Polanski began to assemble his principal players. For Rosemary, he first wanted Sharon Tate's friend Tuesday Weld, best known for her role as Thalia on TV's "Dobbie Gillis." But Paramount wanted Mia Farrow of TV's "Peyton Place" and Frank Sinatra fame. Polanski was unfamiliar with her work, but the moment he saw her—over lunch with Bill Castle—he knew she was perfect. He found himself charmed by her child-ishness, a quality he brings out in the film. As director, Polanski has never been given to explaining motivation. Without psychological explanation, he tells the actor what to do and expects him to do it. Unlike some actresses who have balked at this lack of freedom, Mia Farrow was eager to heed Polanski's orders. Her docility paid off in a brilliant performance.

Polanski wanted Robert Redford for the part of Rose-mary's husband, Guy, but Paramount was about to sue him, which made negotiations sticky. Redford had come to Evans' office to talk unofficially with Castle and Polanski, when a Paramount attorney barged in with a subpoena for him. That killed the casting of Redford, who was furious. Jack Nicholson wanted the role, but Polanski felt he was too little known. Finally, Polanski decided on John Cassa-vetes, after the actor-director suggested himself to Castle.

During shooting, Polanski's choice of Cassavetes proved explosive. Shouting matches broke out between the two, whose mutual dislike grew every day. Cassavetes told the press that he was just trying to stay alive under Polanski's rule. Polanski sarcastically said that he had not been con-cerned with Cassavetes' ability to act. He had been cast, Polanski claimed, to play himself. Polanski saw Guy as a character who was not innately sympathetic.

Seeking revenge for Cassavetes' show of independence during shooting, Polanski even took a cheap shot at his star's impressive directing career: "He isn't a director, he has made some films," Polanski told a French interviewer. "Anyone can take a camera and make a film like he made *Shadows*." Their conflict was philosophical, indicative of two divergent approaches to cinema; Cassavetes wanted more creative space to work in than Polanski was prepared to give.

As Minnie and Roman Castavettes, the witch and war-lock, Polanski chose Ruth Gordon and Sidney Blackmer. With them, he thwarted any assumption on the part of the audience that evil characters would appear grim and sinis-ter. Instead, his witch and warlock are jovial, even zany types, difficult to take seriously as emissaries of Satan. This clever bit of casting contributes to the film's fundamental ambiguity. In Levin's novel, there is no question about the presence of evil forces and their effect on Rosemary. Polanski changes that, leaving everything open to question—till the end.

Ruth Gordon and Polanski adored each other from the moment they met. Polanski played the Beatles' *Lonely Hearts Club Band* for her, winning the veteran actress with boyish charm. Deviating from the novel, he changed Minnie's accent from Midwest flat to New York nasal, thereby anchoring the action in the urban scene. For Polanski, Gordon's verbal *shtik* became an end in itself, not just a means of communicating information.

Part of the shooting took place in New York, at the celebrated Dakota apartment house. Polanski hadn't spent much time in Manhattan, but his acute visual sense gave him the proper feel for detail—assisted by Richard Sylbert, who was a native New Yorker. Polanski aimed at generating a strong tension between the realistic details and the supernatural theme. The story is set in 1965, the year Pope Paul visited New York. Polanski was insistent that the smallest details conform to that year. This was tricky for the designers, since, in effect, it became a period film by only two years. For every bit of furniture or clothing, Polanski wanted proof of accuracy for the period, since he was a foreigner. In 1965 short skirts were becoming fashionable, and women would take up a quarter-inch, then another. Thus costume designer Anthea Sylbert saw to it that, as the film progressed, Rosemary's skirts got shorter and shorter.

Except for the two weeks of location shooting in Manhattan, *Rosemary's Baby* was filmed in the Paramount studios in Los Angeles, mostly on Stage 12. From the first day on the set, the American crew was dazzled by Polanski's technical expertise, the result of his training at Lodz. Polanski and cameraman William Fraker argued constantly—but with mutual respect. Unlike many directors, Polanski knew about optics. He could tell whether a lens was good or not just by holding it—a skill picked up at school. Fraker worked hard to execute Polanski's graphic concepts, and because he wasn't much taller than Polanski, his exceptional utility became obvious: Polanski and the camera looked at things from the same point of view.

The vertiginous dream sequences fracture the film's overall realistic texture and thus posed special aesthetic problems during shooting. The prelude to the rape scene, in which Satan copulates with Rosemary, was filmed on a $150,000 yacht at the Playa Del Ray marina, between Santa Monica and Culver City. Cast and crew eagerly anticipated shooting there as a respite from studio work. For another dream sequence, Polanski ordered a fragment of the ceiling of Michelangelo's Sistine Chapel copied, down to the cracks and discolorations of the original. Artists took six weeks to fabricate the replica.

While shooting the rape, Polanski ordered everyone in the scene to strip, but Cassavetes reminded Polanski that the leading lady was married to Frank Sinatra. Sinatra was angry anyway because, while *Rosemary's Baby* was being shot, Farrow was supposed to be making *The Detective* with him. She thought he would let her finish the Polanski picture, but she was wrong. Shooting took longer than anticipated, and the extra days dragged on. Sinatra called Castle from New York to ask how much longer Polanski would need Farrow. When Castle said three weeks or more, Sinatra replied that Polanski would have to do without her. Panicked, Castle relayed Sinatra's verdict to Polanski. But Farrow had a mind of her own and refused to leave. Sinatra turned up on the set for a final confrontation. The marriage, he told her, was finished.

Sinatra wasn't the only one upset at the production's slow pace. Pressure came from the moguls in New York to speed up. But Polanski remained cool. Confronted by Robert Evans, he agreed that he could go faster but it wouldn't be right. The results would look like a TV series, not the quality film everybody wanted. Evans was convinced. He had looked at the rushes and admired them. He called the money men, taking full responsibility.

The gamble paid off handsomely. "Pray for Rosemary's Baby," announced publicity posters across the country. Levin's best-seller had warmed up the box office. Random House's hard-cover edition had stayed on *The New York Times* Best Sellers list for forty-one weeks, and Dell printed 1.5 million paperbacks to accompany the film's release.

The moral controversy surrounding *Rosemary's Baby* didn't hurt either. The National Catholic Office for Motion Pictures—formerly the Legion of Decency—branded it with a "C" (condemned) rating. "Because of several scenes of nudity," the office stated, "this contemporary horror story about devil worship would qualify for a condemned rating. Much more serious, however, is the perverted use which the film makes of fundamental Christian beliefs, especially the events surrounding the birth of Christ, and its mockery of religious persons and practices. The very technical excellence of the film serves to intensify its defamatory nature." In England, Lord Harlech, president of the Board of Film Censors, acting in conjunction with John Trevelyan, ordered fifteen seconds cut from the rape sequence, because of "elements of kinky sex associated with black magic." In response, Polanski sounded off in the press. "The censors' attitude belongs to the Inquisition," he told the *London Evening Standard.* "But how is the censor going to protect people against all the things they might find kinky?"

The focus of the censorship dispute—the notorious rape by Satan—was a cinematic tour de force in which Polanski replicated the look and feel of irrational dreams. In preparation, he and Sharon discussed their own dreams, attempting to comprehend the mind's elusive mechanisms. He also drew on his own experiences of madness under the influence of LSD. The sequence recalled familiar Polanski preoccupations. A wife is ravished by a monster to whom her husband has given her, suggesting Polanski's recent *Playboy* spread, in which he offered Sharon to the vampire.

Polanski had noticed the absence of sound in his dreams. Thus the rape sequence is silent at first, calling attention to the startling visuals. In a prolonged striptease, Guy undresses the drugged, inert Rosemary, her nakedness observed by the staring witches' coven—and the camera. This is a child's view of sex—a violent act perpetrated by father upon mother. Symbols are inscribed on Rosemary's flesh, in preparation for the beast. When she is tied down, her husband slips away, replaced by Satan, who scratches, then penetrates her.

Polanski had filmed a fantasy-rape before, in *Repulsion.*

Like Carol, Rosemary is childish, immature. Her outfits and manner suggest a little girl. Once she even calls her husband "Daddy." The child's appeal is androgynous: Farrow's Rosemary is a tomboy with gawky legs and overlong, skinny arms. At the moment when she seems most in danger of becoming a full-blown woman—when she discovers her pregnancy—she appears in a boy's haircut, a cap of blond hair.

Rosemary was not an easy role for Mia Farrow. As usual, Polanski was a hard taskmaster. Once, in New York, he commanded her to ignore a red light and dash across a hazardous midtown street while he filmed. Observers speculated that she was channeling personal upset into her performance, since the film had triggered the breakup with Sinatra. She had made a choice that favored her career rather than her husband's wishes. And anxious about Sinatra—thirty years older than she—Farrow became more dependent on Polanski. Because he shot each scene so many times—using her, not a double—she became feverish, and black and blue from rough physical contact.

The depiction of Rosemary's baby—the offspring of the rape—posed a major aesthetic challenge. The novelist suggests with words what each reader fills in for himself. But how can the filmmaker suggest when his camera must show the thing on screen? How could the baby be made horrible enough without seeming ludicrous? Castle suggested using a close-up of a pair of cat's eyes. But Polanski had a subtler idea: keep the baby off screen. Suggest its presence, but never show it. Polanski teases by placing the unseen baby in a bassinet in a crowded room. The witches and warlocks gathered around gaze in. An oriental warlock snaps photos of the scene, presumably capturing on film what Polanski's movie conceals—Rosemary's baby. The trick worked. Some filmgoers vaguely recalled having seen the child's face. When the TV version debuted on ABC, it was reported that censors had deleted shots of the baby.

Rosemary's Baby was a critical and commercial success. Its popularity with audiences was viewed by the moguls as a blow against the Catholic film office. Still, there were a few dissenting voices. In *The New Yorker*, Penelope Gilliatt wrote: "The film is very proficient, but all the same what's it for? If it weren't made by Polanski *(Knife in the Water, Cul de Sac,* and *Repulsion),* I suppose one might not ask the question." And Cassavetes told *Look* magazine: "Ask him why he's so obsessed by the bloody and gruesome, behaving like some kid in a candy store."

All eyes were on Polanski now. It was his show.

eight

WHILE POLANSKI was working on *Rosemary's Baby,* Sharon Tate had gotten her first big break in Hollywood, a role in the movie of Jacqueline Susann's *Valley of the Dolls,* playing an American starlet filmed in the buff by an exploitive European director. The role was a plum for an actress with so little experience, and she was grateful for it. It also meant she would be in Hollywood while Polanski was there. She shared his rented Malibu beach house and worked long hours preparing for the movie.

During shooting, Sharon became friendly with her co-stars Barbara Parkins and Patty Duke, as well as with Susann herself. Sharon confided to Parkins that she was madly in love. Roman could teach her how to live, she said. Parkins noticed the way Sharon gazed at Polanski when they were together. He was her idol. Still, Sharon paid a price for his savoir faire: she had to grant him total sexual freedom. He needed to be able to do as he pleased—without complaint from Sharon. Parkins sensed that Roman was as in love with Sharon as she was with him but couldn't express it as openly as she. Sharon never seemed to grow cynical, even when his life-style made things difficult for her. But she was used to dominant men, for her father had been an intelligence officer in the Army and had ruled the family with military rigidity.

"Yes, there's no doubt that Roman is the man in my life," she told the New York *Sunday News* while making *Valley of the Dolls,* "but neither of us is talking marriage these days. At least, not for a while. I'll tell you one thing though. Should I get married, I guarantee I'll give up my career. It's almost impossible to have a happy marriage and a successful career at the same time. . . ." Questioned about her nude scenes in *The Fearless Vampire Killers* and *Valley of the Dolls,* Sharon insisted that although she was basically a shy person, posing naked for a camera was simply business. "I hope my future assignments call on me to portray sensitive people," she said, "the kind you find in Polanski movies."

Four months after she told the press that she and Roman weren't talking marriage, they arrived in London to wed in a Chelsea registry office. Sharon wore a high-necked mini dress of Victorian taffeta, with girlish ribbons in her hair. Roman was dressed in a tight Edwardian suit, a ruffled ascot around his neck. Every well-oiled hair was in place as he posed stiffly with Sharon for photographers. (Diminutive as the bride was, she was still taller than her husband.) Polanski hadn't exactly proposed to Sharon. When he had mentioned, one day, that he guessed she would like to marry, she said yes. "We'll get married, then," he said. Later, Polanski confided to a friend, "I don't know how she got me to marry her; I don't know how she did it."

After the wedding, Sharon and Roman were fêted by Victor Lownes at the London Playboy Club—still Polanski's favorite hangout. On short notice, Lownes had telegrammed invitations: "You are cordially invited to the Sharon Tate–Roman Polanski wedding reception at the Playboy Club this Saturday January 20 at noon. Informal brunch." The star-studded guest list included Peter Sellers, Laurence Harvey, Rudolf Nureyev, Michael Klinger, Warren Beatty, Prince and Princess Radziwill, Vidal Sassoon, Sean Connery, Kenneth Tynan, David Bailey, Brian Jones, Keith Richard and the British censor John Trevelyan, who had objected to both *Repulsion* and *Rosemary's Baby.*

The Playboy Club had, of course, special significance for Roman and Sharon: "Tate Gallery"—his erotic testament to her—had been published in *Playboy.* And as usual, Lownes was the perfect host, anticipating what he knew would please and amuse his guests. When a cake was wheeled in inscribed (as if the wrong cake had been delivered) "Happy Retirement, Hilda," Polanski looked at it, then roared with laughter. It was, as Sharon told reporters, "a very mod affair."

After the nuptials, the newlyweds jetted between London and Los Angeles. In England they lived in Polanski's tiny mews house off Eaton Square in Belgravia. Photographed by David Bailey (prototype for Antonioni's antihero in *Blow-Up*), Roman and Sharon were the emblematic mod couple, invited everywhere. "The bright young generation in London," said Sharon, "are a bunch of free-thinkers who are feeling their way through life and leaving an impression on the times." In Hollywood the Polanskis took rooms at the arty Chateau Marmont Hotel, then rented a house from Patty Duke. Roman fell in with a fast new Hollywood crowd that included Jack Nicholson, Warren Beatty, Buck Henry, Mike Nichols, Robert Evans, Richard Sylbert and his brother and sister-in-law Paul and Anthea Sylbert—all of whom worked and played together.

The Polanskis also spent much of their time with Jay Sebring. Sharon gave in to Roman on most things but insisted on keeping her ex-lover around. Polanski decided that Sebring was no threat. Still, if Sebring was going to be part of Sharon's life, Polanski wanted to control the situation as much as possible. He decided to cultivate a friendship with the hairdresser, with whom he shared interests in fast cars, the martial arts and women. Sebring was interested in staging sadomasochistic scenes in which he tied naked girls to chairs. But he wasn't always able to bring off the act. One of Sebring's dates, a jaded young lady on the make, grew bored while tied up and laughed openly at her embarrassed tormentor. Afterward she described the scene to friends, to Sebring's humiliation.

Besides hobnobbing with his Hollywood companions, Polanski mingled with the Polish emigrés he had encountered in America. Among them was novelist Jerzy Kosinski, whose *The Painted Bird* and *Steps* had already established his important position in American letters. More successful in adapting to American reality than his old friend, Kosinski maintained a keen interest in Polanski, eventually making him a character in a novel, *Blind Date*. According to Kosinski, Polanski continued to see himself as Polish even though his career had evolved abroad. Polanski felt no need to assimilate, to become an American. Kosinski perceived that America was just another "foreign hotel" to Polanski—as France and England had been.

The contrast between Kosinski and Polanski is instructive, since both are the same age and both left Poland to become major artists in the West. Kosinski realizes that part of his and Polanski's "vision" may be attributed to their youthful wartime experiences, in which they entered into an adversary relationship with their environment. Both Kosinski and Polanski would bring the intensity of violence to their art, frequently creating shocking works riddled with cruelty and perversity. But wisely, Kosinski would assume the acceptable role of moralist and social critic. The Romek in Polanski would never let him do this.

Another of the Polish artists in America was Krzysztof Komeda, Polanski's hero from the jazz sessions at Lodz, who had come to Hollywood with his wife, Zofia, to compose the score for *Rosemary's Baby*. From *Two Men and a Wardrobe* on, Komeda had written the music for all of Polanski's films but *Repulsion*, so when the director went to Hollywood, he wanted Komeda there too. At a birthday party for Komeda attended by Hollywood's colony of Polish artists, Polanski arrived, downed a few drinks, then jumped onto a table and recited lines from *Pan Tadeusz*, the Polish romantic lament for the lost motherland, in which the speaker, a Pole displaced to the streets of Paris, recounts the plight of all such "deserters" who have "fled to foreign climes." Polanski's drunken performance before an audience of fellow "deserters" was shot through with irony. This wasn't Paris; it was Hollywood, a more remote—and grotesque—"foreign clime."

Komeda fell critically ill after an accident, and Polanski became suddenly aloof, hesitant to visit or assist his incapacitated friend. When he did turn up at the hospital, he was so noisy that he was asked to leave. When Komeda won the Golden Globe Award for *Rosemary's Baby*, Polanski sent it to Zofia with a messenger. Attached to it was a calling card on which was written, in a secretary's hand: "Best wishes from the director."

With her husband's death imminent, Zofia took him back to Poland. The night after Komeda's death, Polanski called her. "What can I do for you?" he asked. "At this point," Zofia replied, "it is *I* who can help you. If you haven't turned into an animal yet, I recommend that you try to become a human being again."

Of the Poles who had gathered in Hollywood, the one closest to Polanski wasn't an artist at all—the former Lodz playboy Wojtek Frykowski. Having left Poland, Frykowski no longer had lots of money. Polanski was his big contact in the West, and he had come to California to collect on the debt Romek owed him for having produced *Mammals*. Frykowski was a large, witty man—and Polanski liked having him around for kicks. But he was ambivalent about his old buddy and alternated between warmth and hostility, sometimes treating him like a hanger-on as the unemployed Frykowski became more and more a fixture in his life. By all accounts, Polanski seemed worried that people would think he was permitting Frykowski to exploit him.

Before turning up in Hollywood, Frykowski had stopped in New York, where Jerzy Kosinski, eager to assist him, offered to introduce him to well-to-do women. (Kosinski knew something about them, having been married for six years to Mary Hayward Weir, widow of a steel magnate and ten years his senior.) One of the names on Kosinski's list was Abigail "Gibby" Folger, a studious, plain-looking coffee heiress. Gibby quickly became involved with the outrageous, muscular Pole, who called her "Lady Folger" and, because of his halting English, conversed with her mostly in French. He told her he was on his way to Hollywood to see his friend Romek Polanski. He bragged that he had worked as Polanski's assistant on *Knife in the Water*, exaggerating his peripheral function as a swimming coach. Gibby was fascinated, as earlier she had been by Kosinski. Coming as she did from a sheltered world of debutante parties and football players, she found Frykowski and Kosinski different—more sophisticated. The American blueblood warmed to their promise of worldliness.

In August 1968, Wojtek and Gibby left for California. In Hollywood, he finally "caught" Romek—as friends joked —but Wojtek remained unemployed. He and Gibby made friends with Jay Sebring, and she invested about $3,500—

a small sum, considering her fortune—in Sebring International, Jay's haircutting chain. Sebring and his black Porsche were easily recognized on the Hollywood scene, and consequently he felt he needed someone to make his drug pickups for him. Frykowski explained to Kosinski why he could best handle Jay's drug deals—since he was new in town and unknown—making the pickups in a Peugeot.

Sharon and Gibby became fast friends. According to Kosinski, the women got along so well because "they shared impossible conditions, two egocentric narcissists. Each one contributed knowledge of her own difficulty to the other." Although Polanski and Frykowski liked to spend time with girls, Kosinski says that neither was *really* a ladies' man. Instead, both were narcissists seeking "blind adoration without any effort."

Polanski and his entourage of the famous and not-so-famous mixed easily into the newly emerging casual lifestyle of late-sixties California, still under the spell of the hippies and "the summer of love." The Polanski household was soon known as one of the most *open* spots in town. According to the media-hyped hippie ethic—increasingly popular in the movie colony—it was uncool to check guest lists, uptight to exclude street people. Polanski—described by Kosinski as "situational"—became immersed in the visual and auditory aspects of the milieu, not with its implications or consequences. As a foreigner, Polanski couldn't always read his guests and relied on Sharon to make sense of who and what they were. Unfortunately, she was too naive and friendly to monitor the people they dealt with. A friend describes her as "just so open," inhabiting "a wonderful, little fantasy" in which everything was "soft and flowing." Polanski's more conventional friends were sometimes alarmed by what they began to find at his home. One night, when the suave, courtly composer Bronislaw Kaper attended a gathering there, he was disconcerted when a seedy-looking crasher asked him whose house this was—and whose party.

In 1968, Polanski, now a successful, sought-after director, was invited to France, to sit on the jury of the Cannes Film Festival, where, not long before, *Repulsion* and *Cul de Sac* had each been refused for competition. But the times were

A holiday excursion to Wawel Castle, Cracow, Poland, 1946. But this quartet is no ordinary group of children on an outing. All four are Jewish survivors of the Nazi holocaust. Roman Polanski, aged 13, small for his age, appears at the upper right. At the end of the war, he made his way back from the countryside where he had been hiding from the Nazis and was reunited with his father, a concentration camp survivor. Romek's mother had perished in Auschwitz. Seated next to Romek is Bronislawa Horowitz, also 13. The boy in the sailor suit is Romek's playmate, Ryszard Horowitz, aged 6, who was incarcerated in Auschwitz from the age of 2 until 5. The girl in the sailor suit is Romek's cousin, Roma Ligocka, then 7.

ABOVE Romek, aged 26, as a student at the celebrated Lodz film school. He had discovered that directing allowed him to stage his imaginative world. Here he proudly poses on the set where he was making one of his early student films, *The Lamp* (1959). Directly to his right in the back row is his first wife, Poland's first movie star, Barbara Kwiatkowska (Basia), aged 19. To his left, in the light jacket, is Adam Holender, a fellow student and today a Hollywood cinematographer.

BELOW LEFT A taut drama of sexual rivalry and humiliation, *Knife in the Water* (1962), marked Polanski's debut as a feature director. He is said to have considered the film his "ticket to the West." To the left is Zygmunt Malanowicz; on the right is Leon Niemczyk.

BELOW RIGHT Jerzy Skolimowski, coauthor of the screenplay of *Knife in the Water*. When Polanski was unable to play the role of the handsome young boy, he asked Skolimowski. That idea failed too, and he cast Malanowicz, who, with bleached hair, could pass on the screen for Skolimowski's twin. Today Skolimowski is an important international director.

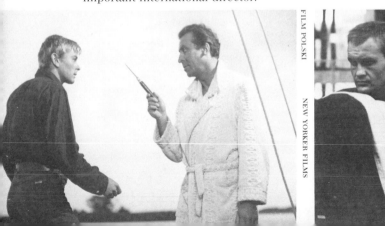

Polanski (left) and novelist Jerzy Kosinski (right), two of Poland's best-known artistic exports. Kosinski is introducing Polanski to Nobel Prize–winner Dr. Jacques Monod at the Cannes Film Festival in May 1976.

THE POLISH CULTURAL MILIEU

Polanski in 1977, on his first visit to Poland in nearly 15 years. He was frequently attacked for having abandoned his Polish identity. From left to right: director Janusz Majewski, his film school roommate; Polanski; Janusz Morgenstern, a director and his host on this visit; Andrzej Wajda, Poland's most acclaimed director; Jerzy Mierzejiewski, his former professor at Lodz.

Looking . . .
(Catherine Deneuve in *Repulsion*, 1965) (*Repulsion*, 1965)

. . . at himself
(Polanski in *The Tenant*, 1976)

THE ENIGMA OF VIOLENCE OBSERVED

Polanski's films are not merely about violence, but violence *observed*, the allure of base acts. This preoccupation with voyeurism and violence is the most elemental force in his cinema.

A RECURRENT FANTASY

Polanski has pictured each of his great loves—Basia Kwiat-kowska, Sharon Tate and Nastassia Kinski—in the same way: gazing out through a window. He has also envisioned himself in this position. For Polanski, looking—and being looked at—are erotic acts.

Basia Kwiatkowska in
When Angels Fall (1959).

Sharon Tate in
The Fearless Vampire Killers (1967).

Polanski in *The
Fearless Vampire Killers.*

Polanski in *The Tenant* (1976).

Nastassia Kinski in *Tess* (1979).

Polanski and Sharon Tate at their marriage in London, January 1968.

"I am the man of the spectacle." (Roman Polanski, 1977)

Polanski with Mia Farrow on the set of *Rosemary's Baby* (1968), the day her hair was cut.

Polanski and Sharon Tate.

His friend Victor Lownes supports the grief-stricken Polanski as he arrives by plane in Los Angeles after the murder of Sharon Tate and several friends in August 1969.

THE
VICTIMIZED
CHILD

In *Chinatown* (1974), Faye Dunaway played Evelyn Mulwray, the tortured victim of an incestuous father.

The conclusion of *Chinatown* was scripted by Polanski himself. Conventionally, detective stories end in the restitution of social order as subversive elements are dispelled. In Polanski's travesty of the genre, violence and desire triumph: Evelyn Mulwray is killed by a cop, and her father, Noah Cross, claims the child-victim she had sought to protect.

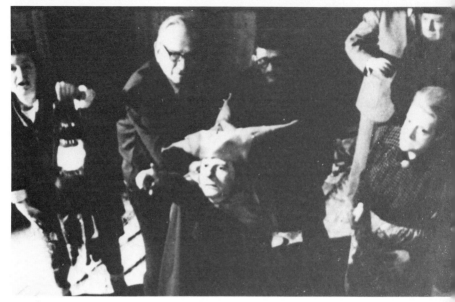

In *The Tenant*, the child-victim—wearing a Polanski-mask and jester's cap—points accusingly at him as he watches her from a window above. She cries out in his voice. This is an ironic self-portrait: a revelation of Romek's identification with the tiny, victimized child.

Polanski is arrested in 1977 on charges of having had sexual relations with a 13-year-old California schoolgirl.

IMAGES OF HIMSELF

(The Tenant)

AS VICTIM

(The Fearless Vampire Killers)

(Two Men and a Wardrobe)

AS VICTIMIZER

(Chinatown)

Polanski's interest in drag reflects an inclination to experiment with identity. In *When Angels Fall*, he shared a female role with his first wife, Basia Kwiatkowska.

In June 1981, Polanski returned to Poland to direct and costar, as Mozart, in Peter Schaffer's play, *Amadeus*.

During a visit to New York in 1965, Polanski embraces a monster.

Polanski caused an uproar in Cannes in May 1979 when he kissed
the youthful Nastassia Kinski before the press.

". . . normal love isn't interesting. I assure you that it's incredibly boring." (Roman Polanski, 1977).

A few months after Polanski was arrested on a sex charge, a photographer spotted him chatting with some young girls in Saint-Tropez. A police car happened along and he jogged off.

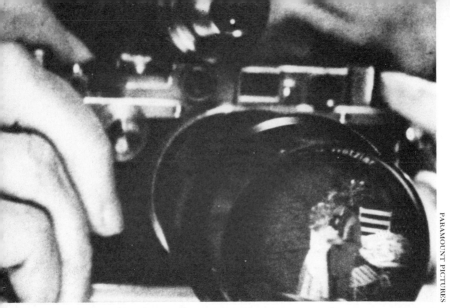

In Polanski's emblematic image, from *Chinatown*, Jack Nicholson's camera reflects an illicit scene involving a young girl and an older man.

Polanski may be the cinema's most visible director. (Brazil, 1981)

against Polanski now that he had made it, for in 1968 violence was in the air. Simultaneously with Cannes, students were at the barricades in Paris engaging in politically motivated confrontations with armed authorities. In the sunny south of France, leading directors moved to shut down the festival in a gesture of solidarity with the struggling students.

Polanski arrived, excited by his success and his new-found status, to find everyone else swept away by the radical fervor of the moment. When fellow directors proposed to cancel the activities, Polanski halfheartedly agreed. *Variety* reported that "Polanski did feel that perhaps more could be gained by finishing the fest and giving unorthodox prizes to remove the idea of 'commercialism' at fests. But he went along." In Poland, he had been considered too apolitical. Now, in the West, leftist politics threatened him again. The radical French directors' group, the Etats Generaux, proposed worker control of cinema. But Polanski had left Poland to escape this kind of regulation. He wanted to work in a commercial cinema, not a nationalized one. "I never intended my pulling out to be seen as an anti-Cannes gesture," he said later. "People like Truffaut, Lelouch and Godard are like little kids playing at being revolutionaries. I've passed through this stage. I lived in a country where these things happened seriously."

These directors, moreover, were the people who hadn't helped Polanski when he first made the rounds in Paris. Now a prominent director himself, Polanski had looked forward to donning a tuxedo at the festival. Instead, he found Lelouch and Truffaut spoiling the party, arguing against tuxedos as snobbish. The scruffy, drably dressed Jean-Luc Godard had little patience for Polanski, decked out in trendy Sunset Strip attire. "I wanted to make myself clear at the time," Polanski complained, "but whenever I'd open my mouth to say anything, Godard would interrupt me."

Disappointed and in conflict, Polanski returned to the States, where violence hit the headlines with the shooting of Andy Warhol and of Robert Kennedy. Lamenting the Warhol attack to Archer Winsten, Polanski said that "everybody here has a gun." One of the grips on the Hollywood set for *Rosemary's Baby* had given Polanski a Colt .45. Having practiced with it regularly, Polanski quipped that he had become the "fastest Pole in the West." But Polanski had other things on his mind than violence. More compelling were his Ferrari, his beautiful bride and the other girls who—five months after the wedding—were still very much a part of his life.

nine

FOR HIS NEXT project, Polanski teamed up with Gerard Brach to write a script, *A Day at the Beach,* based on a Dutch novel by Heere Heresma. Suddenly, Polanski discovered, he had clout in Hollywood: on his recommendation MGM hired a young Moroccan friend of his, Simon Hesera, to direct the movie, which featured Peter Sellers and was produced by Polanski and Gutowski's Cadre Films. Meanwhile, he worked up ideas for two other projects—a film about Paganini and a western about cannibalism, *Donner's Pass.* But these were put off in favor of *The Day of the Dolphin,* which he signed to script and direct for United Artists.

He decided to work on the screenplay in the London mews house where he had written *Rosemary's Baby.* Meanwhile, Sharon would go to Rome to star in a new movie, *Twelve + One Chairs,* and the couple would commute between England and Italy. Preparing to leave for Rome, Sharon found out that she was pregnant. Thrilled at the news, but anxious about her husband's reaction, she didn't tell him right away. She confided in a friend that she thought Roman hadn't wanted a baby. When she did tell him, the idea at first scared him, connoting as it did the "nest" he had long avoided. But in time he grew enthusiastic about Sharon's pregnancy, talking of his excitement with Michael Klinger and others. He and Sharon were hoping for a girl.

Filming in Rome, Sharon tried to conceal the tummy that was beginning to form. She and Polanski wanted the baby to be born in America, so when she was four months pregnant, she flew to Los Angeles to look for a place larger than the one they were leasing from Patty Duke. She located a $200,000 house for rent on Cielo Drive in Benedict Canyon; its current tenant was Terry Melcher, Doris Day's son.

99

Unable to decide, Sharon called Polanski's agent, Bill Tennant, and asked him to judge whether or not Roman would like it. When he got there, Tennant was effusive. There was a wishing well, a swimming pool, a loft in the living room, and a room that Tennant figured would make a perfect nursery.

The Polanskis moved to Cielo Drive on February 15, 1969. A month later they gave a housewarming party. The arrival of some crashers led to an argument and their expulsion. At Cielo Drive, Roman and Sharon continued to be popular hosts, although some friends still worried about the strange types who continued to turn up at their parties. Polanski had begun to cultivate a new technological toy— video tape—which appealed to his director's instinct. Sexual scenes were staged and taped, to be played and replayed. The tapes, eventually seized by police, depicted well-known Hollywood figures at play—including Roman and Sharon. Some time later, Polanski would tell that most cerebral of voyeurs, Andy Warhol, that he had little interest in pornographic films like *Deep Throat*. He might be more interested, he suggested, in watching *himself* engaged in sexual acts. Video tape permitted Polanski this subtle, reflexive pleasure, coupling voyeurism and narcissism.

In March 1969, before Sharon returned to Rome to finish shooting—Polanski had already gone back to England—a hippie turned up at her door. When asked what he wanted, he replied that he was looking for Terry Melcher. Theatrical agent Rudi Altobelli, owner of the house, happened to be there at the time, and he recognized the short, slightly built hippie and sent him away. For a moment, Sharon Tate had come face to face with Charles Manson.

The Polanskis had arranged for English director Michael Sarne to occupy the house while they were away. But the plans fell through, and the house was offered to Wojtek and Gibby, then renting a more modest place on Woodstock Road. Frykowski jumped at the chance. By this time he was moving without caution in the subterranean drug culture, mingling with people he neither understood nor took seriously. Now he could invite them to see him in Roman Polanski's house. Confronted by American hippies, he found, as had Polanski, that it wasn't easy to tell whether they were harmless college kids or hardcore criminal types, for the dress and manner of the period blurred what distinctions there were between them. Like Polanski, Frykowski was a foreigner who didn't quite comprehend the milieu in which he found himself, who couldn't read the danger signs.

Still unemployed, Wojtek told people that he was doing research for Polanski's current project. At Cielo Drive, he was constantly on the phone, making what he claimed were business deals, presumably in film. His friend, the Polish emigré painter Witold Kaczanowski, found Frykowski succumbing to insatiable curiosity and injudicious experimentation with mescaline and other drugs.

Matters in the Polanski household were growing increasingly out of control. In the driveway one day, Wojtek accidentally ran over and killed Sharon's Yorkshire, Dr. Sapirstein, named after one of the warlocks in *Rosemary's Baby*. Gibby had been doing some social work and participated in the Los Angeles campaign of black mayoral candidate Thomas Bradley. She might have been expected to guide Wojtek in his dealings with people and drugs, but she too was out of her depth, as lost as he. Unattractive, torn by guilt feelings about her wealth and the way she was living, Gibby became increasingly subservient to Frykowski's strong hand.

In London, Polanski was eagerly anticipating the prospect of fatherhood. He had lunch with Michael Klinger at the Polish Club in Kensington and said that he had never been so happy in his life. He felt that his life was finally coming together emotionally. By mid-July 1969, Sharon was more than eight months pregnant, and the airlines would no longer permit her to fly. Polanski was too restless for an ocean journey, so Sharon took the voyage home alone. He would, he promised, follow a few days later by plane. First, more work needed to be done on the script for *The Day of the Dolphin*. Sharon departed on the *Queen Elizabeth II*, accompanied by a new puppy called Prudence, which Roman had given her to replace Dr. Sapirstein.

Polanski didn't return to Los Angeles as promised but remained in London writing and vigorously socializing.

Back home, Sharon awaited his return and prepared for giving birth, purchasing baby clothes and books on child care. In the final stages of pregnancy, she didn't want to stay in the house alone, so Wojtek and Gibby were invited to keep her company.

On August 8, at about eleven in the morning, Sharon received a call from Roman in London. He assured her that he would fly to California the following week in time for the baby's arrival and his thirty-sixth birthday on August 18. In London, Polanski had finished a day's work, and when he said good-bye to Sharon, he set off for dinner with Victor Lownes. At the evening's end, Polanski went home to bed with a girl Lownes classified as a "bimbo." Lownes never quite got her name.

At Cielo Drive, two of Sharon's girlfriends dropped by for lunch. Mrs. Winifred Chapman, the Polanskis' maid, arrived, did some housework and left. Sharon later telephoned novelist Jacqueline Susann—with whom she had become friendly while making *Valley of the Dolls*—and asked her to drop by for cocktails. Learning that critic Rex Reed was visiting Susann, she invited him as well, but the two writers decided to go directly to dinner, forgoing drinks at the Polanskis'.

At about six that evening Wojtek turned up at Kaczanowski's new art gallery in the Beverly Wilshire Hotel and invited him out to dinner with Gibby, Sharon and Jay, then to Cielo Drive for drugs. The gallery was being readied for its opening, and Kaczanowski passed up the invitation in order to continue laying carpet. "I just bought myself new pants," said Frykowski, referring to his pink flower-patterned trousers. "If you want to be a fag," Kaczanowski replied, "go ahead. But the fags are going to be after you." Before he left, Frykowski told Kaczanowski that he was in the ninth day of a continuous mescaline trip.

Frykowski called the artist later to invite him again, but Kaczanowski again declined. He said he and his girlfriend, Christine Larene, might drop by at Cielo Drive afterward. Frykowski also called another Polish friend for dinner, Professor Stanislaw Wohl, one of Polanski's teachers at Lodz. But Wohl said that he was dining with composer Bronislaw Kaper. Since Wohl was leaving for New York the next day, after eight days in California, Frykowski asked him to stop at Cielo Drive so Sharon could say good-bye. Frykowski said that Wohl would have to take a cab, since Frykowski was on drugs and wouldn't be able to pick him up. The Kaper dinner lasted till the early hours of the morning, and Wohl never got to Cielo Drive.

When Jay Sebring appeared at the house, he, Wojtek, Sharon and Gibby left for dinner at the El Coyote Restaurant. Then they returned home. Eventually Gibby retired to a bedroom, Jay accompanied Sharon to hers, and Wojtek crashed on the American-flag-draped couch in the living room.

Late that night, at the Beverly Wilshire, Witold Kaczanowski and Christine Larene finished laying the carpet in the gallery. On the way home, he contemplated a stop at Cielo Drive but decided to turn in with Christine instead.

ten

WHEN THE MAID, Mrs. Chapman, arrived the next morning, August 9, she found the bodies. Later, William Tennant, Polanski's agent, received a call from his wife. Sharon's mother had contacted her, having gotten word from one of Jay Sebring's business associates that something was wrong at Cielo Drive. Tennant drove to the house to find out what had happened. When he got there, police asked him to identify the bodies—Tate, Folger, Frykowski and Sebring. A fifth corpse discovered in a car outside the house was unknown to him. Appalled at what he had seen, Tennant vomited when he left the house, then rushed to his car and drove away. Gathered outside, alerted by the police radio, reporters figured that something unspeakable had occurred within.

Tennant called Polanski in London and broke the news: Sharon and the others were dead. At first Polanski envisioned a mudslide, but Tennant said it had been murder. Two friends were with Polanski when Tennant called— Andrew Braunsberg and Michael Brown. Polanski wandered the London streets for a while. When he got back to the mews house, a doctor gave him an injection so that he might sleep.

Autopsies provided some idea of what had gone on. The boy in the car whom Tennant couldn't identify was eighteen-year-old Steven Parent, who had been visiting caretaker William Garretson in another small house on the grounds. Parent had been shot three times in the chest and once in the face. Frykowski and Folger were also outside, having managed to flee the house. Her white nightdress dyed with blood, Folger had twenty-eight stab wounds. Frykowski, who appeared to have put up a ferocious struggle, had fifty-one stab wounds and two gunshot wounds. His head had been bashed thirteen times with a blunt object, later revealed to be the gun handle. In Gibby Folger's system at the time of her death were 2.4 milligrams of methylenedioxyamphetamine (MDA); there were 0.6 milligrams of the same drug in Frykowski's. Sharon Tate, eight and a half months pregnant, had sixteen stab wounds, in the chest and back, piercing heart, lungs and liver. She was found, clad in panties and bra, a rope looped around her neck and strung across a rafter on the ceiling, joining her to Jay Sebring, whose neck was also tied. Sprawled on the floor before the fireplace, Sebring had been shot once and stabbed seven times.

Polanski flew back to Los Angeles, accompanied by Victor Lownes and Gene Gutowski. When, supported by the towering figure of Lownes, Polanski, eyes shrouded in dark glasses, got off the plane in Los Angeles, he was quickly driven to the seclusion of an apartment on the grounds of Paramount Studios. No one yet knew who had murdered his wife and friends, and it was feared that Polanski might also be a target. The apartment inside the studio gates would be more secure than a hotel.

The tension in Hollywood was exacerbated by another multiple murder, twenty-four hours after the slaughter on Cielo Drive. Grocer Leno LaBianca and his wife, Rosemary, were found slashed to death only nine miles away. If the two crimes were linked, the range of possible suspects in the Tate murder broadened far beyond the Polanski circle, for the two households had nothing to do with each other.

Still, all leads had to be pursued, all conceivable motives. The two cases might not be connected after all. At first even Polanski had to be cleared, although he had been thousands of miles away at the time: killers might have been hired. Polanski was convinced that someone in his circle was responsible and began to conduct his own investigation, sometimes openly, sometimes in secret. The clue he focused on initially was something the killers had scrawled on the door of his house: the word "PIG"—in Sharon's blood, as it later turned out. When producer Bill Castle visited at Paramount, Polanski gave him a piece of paper and asked him to write "PIG."

After the discovery of the bodies, the police had arrested

William Garretson, the nineteen-year-old caretaker at Cielo Drive, the only person remaining alive on the hill. He had been found in the caretaker's cottage, alive and completely unharmed, claiming that he hadn't heard a thing all night. It soon became clear that Garretson was not the murderer, and he was released. The investigation was pursuing other, seemingly more promising leads.

When Kaczanowski and Christine arrived at the gallery at the Beverly Wilshire and heard about the massacre, the artist panicked. Images of two recent incidents came to mind. About two weeks before, Sebring had called Polanski to ask permission to give a business party at Cielo Drive. Polanski agreed. For the party, the house was packed with guests, including celebrities like Warren Beatty and John Phillips. The usual crashers also turned up. Polanski had asked that Frykowski and Kaczanowski control any incidents. So when Frykowski noticed two drunks pushing their way through the crowd and insulting people, he called Kaczanowski. Meanwhile, one of the drunks obscenely rubbed against a female guest. Kaczanowski stopped him: "If you're not going to behave, you have to leave the house." Provoked, the two drunks were ready for a fight. Frykowski and Kaczanowski called the bartenders to help eject the troublemakers. Outside, as the gate closed, one of the drunks muttered, "You fucking son of a bitch. We'll be back and we'll kill you!"

Then Kaczanowski thought of a violent fight he had had three weeks before with a young friend of Frykowski's named "Pic." When Frykowski took over at Cielo Drive, Kaczanowski moved into the house on Woodstock Road rented by Gibby. Trouble broke out when Frykowski let Pic stay there as well. Pic had been the boyfriend of *zaftig* Mama Cass Elliot, of the Mamas and the Papas—who lived across the street on Woodstock Road—and Frykowski had introduced him to Polanski and Sharon Tate. Forced together, Pic and Kaczanowski didn't get along. Pic moved out of the house, angry at Frykowski and Kaczanowski. The word "PIG" had been scrawled on the door at Cielo Drive. But the "G" had been unclear. It might have been "C"— "PIC."

Convinced that somewhere in these memories lay the

key to the murders, Kaczanowski was paralyzed by fear. It was he who provided the police with their original direction in the investigation—one which proved eventually to be false. But Kaczanowski didn't go directly to the police. He was afraid for his life, but he was also in the country illegally, his visa having run out. He first fled to the house of John Phillips, Polanski's friend and a former member of the Mamas and the Papas. From there Kaczanowski called the journalist David Halberstam in New York to seek advice. Halberstam realized that an expired visa was the least of Kaczanowski's worries. It was Halberstam who, through the Los Angeles bureau of *The New York Times,* arranged for the police to pick up Kaczanowski and his girlfriend. Reassured by Halberstam, Kaczanowski went with the police, who escorted the pair to Paramount Studios, where Polanski was secluded. When they got there, Gutowski was with Polanski, who soon went to bed. Kaczanowski positioned himself at the bedroom door and watched, with morose fascination, as Polanski jerked repeatedly in agitated dreams. Authorities decided to move Kaczanowski and Larene to a different hotel each night while the leads he offered were checked.

Sharon Tate was buried on Wednesday, August 13. With her was the body of her "perfectly formed," unborn son, whom Polanski had named "Richard Paul"—after his father, Ryszard Polanski, and hers, Colonel Paul Tate. Sharon's family came to Holy Cross Cemetery, as did leading Hollywood figures like Yul Brynner, Steve McQueen, Warren Beatty, John Phillips and Peter Sellers—all frequent guests at the Polanski household. Although the coffin was closed, Sharon was buried in a Pucci mini dress selected from her closet by Victor Lownes. After the services, guests attended an "after the funeral brunch" at Robert Evans' home.

Jay Sebring was buried the same day at Forest Lawn cemetery, after a funeral attended by celebrity clients, business associates and friends. Gibby Folger was buried by her parents in a Catholic service in San Francisco. Steven Parent, the young victim who had never even been inside the Polanski household, was buried by family and friends.

Only Wojtek Frykowski remained unburied. Since Frykowski had no family in the United States, David Halberstam had suggested to his Polish wife, a longtime friend of Frykowski's, that she and Jerzy Kosinski make things easier for Polanski by handling his friend's funeral. On August 11, the Monday after the killings, Kosinski called from New York to say that he would arrange for Frykowski's burial. But when Frykowski's mother was reached in Poland by phone, she insisted that she and Frykowski's brother would fly to America to claim the body.

The press carried reports that Kosinski had been due at Cielo Drive on August 9. Kosinski said that Frykowski had invited him to come from Paris. But when Kosinski's luggage was sent to New York by mistake, he didn't get to Los Angeles and missed the slaughter. Witold Kaczanowski, once Kosinski's friend, scoffed at these reports. Kosinski, he claimed, wasn't expected that night and was merely seeking publicity.

Victor Lownes was also disturbed by Kosinski's statements—but for different reasons. Polanski was sure the killers were among his acquaintances, and Lownes grew suspicious of Kosinski. On the Monday after the murders, Lownes had spoken by phone with Kosinski about arrangements for Frykowski's burial. The writer had not mentioned anything to Lownes about having had plans to be at Cielo Drive on August 9. When Lownes picked up the newspapers and saw Kosinski telling interviewers that he had narrowly escaped death because his luggage had been misdirected, he was perplexed. Other, absolutely innocent things Kosinski had done began to seem sinister—like his calling Lownes back to say that Frykowski's family was coming from Poland and that they, not Kosinski, would arrange for the disposition of the body.

Back in London, on August 22, Lownes sent a letter to the L.A. Homicide Division suggesting they question Kosinski. On the flight back to London, Lownes, devouring Kosinski's *Steps*, had become fascinated with the book's violent imagery. What mind, he wondered, was capable of this? And what would such a mind be capable of in life? (The question has been asked about writers from the Marquis de Sade to William Burroughs.) To Lownes, the killings seemed to spring from the pages of Kosinski's novel, whose ideas and impulses they realized. In the letter, Lownes said that he had been struck by what he called Kosinski's "preoccupation with 'pointless' murder, and the bizarre notion of someone achieving a kind of freedom by preparing themselves for pure violence and absolute sexuality." The fact that the book was written in "the first person" added to Lownes's discomfort. He had been taken in by Kosinski's device of blurring the boundaries between fiction and life. Lownes asked, "Is it just remotely possible that the author of such weird material might himself be a very weird person indeed?" Half embarrassed about having written, Lownes concluded, "I know that the suggestion is extremely far-fetched, but surely it is worth while to check on the mixed-up luggage story, the change in plans on the funeral of Voityck [sic], and Kosinski's whereabouts over that terrible week-end. Meantime, I hope you've solved the crime and it won't even be necessary to go into this line of (un)reasoning. . . ." Such speculation was, in fact, unfounded, and no link or even implication of a link between Kosinski and the murders was ever found.

Farfetched as it is—and Lownes was the first to admit it —the letter is significant because it indicates how easy it is, with a writer like Kosinski, to confuse art and life, to assume that the author is fully capable of living out his darkest literary scenarios. Because Kosinski, like Polanski, has keyed his work to the audience's consciousness of his image, he has subtly encouraged—even made inevitable —this confusion of art and life, while deriding it in his interviews.

This confusion was evident in the press coverage of the crimes, in which the slaughter at Cielo Drive seemed to come from a Polanski film, as if Polanski had somehow brought the tragedy upon himself. The overwhelming strangeness of the events was made comprehensible by depicting them with reference to the director's world. Describing the Polanski home after the crime, *Time* stated, on August 15: "It was a scene as grisly as anything depicted in Polanski's film explorations of the dark and melancholy corners of the human character." In an article titled "The Hollywood Murders," *Newsweek* said, on August 18: "The scene could hardly have been more bizarre had it appeared in one of Polish director Roman Polanski's own peculiarly nightmarish motion pictures." Then *Newsweek* went on to describe the scene as if it were a film: "Had there been cameras rolling as the door swung open, they would have captured the most chilling sight of all. A gorgeous blonde, clad only in panties and a bra, lay brutally knifed on the giant living room floor. A white nylon cord ran around her neck, over a ceiling beam, then to the neck of yet another bloody body, its head shrouded in blood. But this was no film, the house no set." The camera metaphor establishes a comforting distance from the view. So vivid—and startling —are the details of violence that they must seem to have been filmed, then coldly scrutinized on a screen. Only after the camera metaphor has been established can the shock of reality intrude. Closing, *Newsweek* returned to its metaphor in a final reference to Sharon Tate: "In the end, she took the lead role in a murder mystery far more tragic and macabre than Polanski could ever have crafted for her on the screen. 'Man,' gasped one detective, 'this is weirder than *Rosemary's Baby.*' "

For *Time,* a few days before, the killings had been "as grisly as" Polanski's films. Now *Newsweek* concluded that the crimes outdid Polanski. Next, on August 22, *Time*'s coverage outdid the killings, making them even grislier and sicker than they were. Even the eminently respectable national newsweekly inadvertently was taken in briefly by some of the more grotesque rumors then circulating everywhere in Los Angeles. Mistaken details of sexual mutilation were added to the depiction: "Sharon's body was found nude, not clad in bikini pants and bra as had first been reported. Sebring was wearing only the torn remnants of a pair of boxer shorts. One of Miss Tate's breasts had been cut off, apparently as a result of indiscriminate slashing. She was nine months pregnant, and there was an X cut on her stomach. What appeared to be the bloody handle of a paring knife was found next to her leg, the blade broken off. Sebring had been sexually mutilated and his body also bore X marks." Describing Sharon Tate and Jay Sebring like this, in a single paragraph, with analogous details, suggested a relationship between them, a rumor the press was abuzz with. In a news conference, Polanski lashed out at such insinuations by the press. Later, bitterly, he would say, "God*damn* them! The victims were assassinated two times: once by the murderers, the second time by the press."

When Polanski permitted a *Life* correspondent and a photographer to accompany him and medium Peter Hurkos to Cielo Drive, he sought to dispel speculation about Sharon and Jay. Talking to correspondent Thomas Thompson, Polanski offered his version of events as he looked over the house for the first time since returning to Los Angeles. "Sharon must have been asleep that night," Polanski told Thompson as they entered the master bedroom. "Look, there, the pillows—she always put them that way when I was gone." Thompson noted that only one side of the bed had been slept on. "She hugged the pillows instead of me," Polanski said. "She must have been awakened by the noise and got up." Polanski's scenario suggested that his wife had been alone that night, while subsequent testimony by the killers would indicate that Sebring was in the room with her. Entering Frykowski's bedroom, Polanski told Thompson: "I should have thrown him out when he ran over Sharon's dog." Questioned about how long Frykowski and Folger had been in the house, Polanski responded, "Too long, I guess." Kosinski was annoyed by Polanski's public attitude toward Frykowski. Kosinski figured that by making Frykowski a scapegoat, Polanski hoped that attention would be deflected from Sebring and his relationship with Sharon.

On August 29, Polanski appeared in a color photo in *Life*. Beneath the heading, "A Tragic Trip to the House on the Hill," Polanski was pictured sitting on the blood-spattered front porch of his house, the door ajar, leading to the ruin within. The photograph was not spontaneous but staged. Although Polanski was in front of the camera, not behind it, he was in control. To some people in Hollywood, this behavior was grotesque. To Kosinski, it was Polanski's attempt to "direct," but the attempt "backfired." Permitting himself to be photographed like this was Polanski's strategy for mastering what had happened. But Polanski was no longer in control of the image he had created for himself.

In the coverage of the murders, his image became a media property; his image linked him to violence, an association that he had long cultivated on screen and that resulted in the tastelessness of the media coverage with its recurrent references to his films.

Hoping to allay suspicion about himself, Polanski agreed to submit to a lie-detector test, in which he discussed his relationship with Sharon, how he met her and her connection with Sebring. He also speculated on the reason for the murder. If the murderers had been at the house looking for someone specific, Polanski was certain that it couldn't have been Sharon. She was one person no one could have had a grudge against. Either Sebring or Polanski would have been more likely targets. At the time he took the lie-detector test, Polanski had already begun to doubt the idea that the killings were connected to narcotics. This was the theory the police were currently favoring, and Polanski demurred, explaining to the polygraph investigator that something more "illogical" was at the crime's source. Test results convinced police that Polanski knew nothing about the killings.

He was, however, obsessed with finding some clue. After his first visit to Cielo Drive, with the *Life* crew, he returned several times as if there might be some explanation hidden there for what had happened. He had moved from the apartment at the Paramount Studios to Robert Evans' home, which had been surrounded with round-the-clock armed protection. Polanski was making every effort to keep his suspicions and his investigations to himself, as he told the police, largely because he continued to believe it was someone he and Sharon knew. His closest friends quickly learned that it was best to amuse him, to divert him with restaurants and company rather than drawn-out condolences.

Polanski was not the only one to feel himself in danger. Overnight, or so it seemed to many people, the open lifestyle of the sixties came to an end. Richard Sylbert remarked to a friend as he landed in Los Angeles after the murders, "You can hear the toilets flushing all over Beverly Hills." For Sylbert, all at once, "Everybody became Presbyterian. That marked the end of the fun and games of the 60s. . . . It was the end of the joke."

Monday, August 18, was Roman Polanski's thirty-sixth birthday. On the following day, he flew to Jamaica, the West Indies, with John Phillips to scout locations for *The Day of the Dolphin,* but also to find out about Frykowski's drug connections there. The trip, however, was abortive on both counts. Polanski dropped his film project, unable to concentrate sufficiently to work. He had found no clues.

Leaving Jamaica at the end of August, Polanski flew to New York, where he knew he could see friends. He stayed, as he usually did, at the Essex House on Central Park South and was seen about town with friends: lunching at P. J. Clarke's with columnist Steve Brandt, visiting Warren Beatty at the Delmonico. But after a few days, New York had begun to seem like a "peep show" to him, his every move being watched. Richard Sylbert, who was with him in the city, realized that Polanski had suddenly become "the most well-known motion picture director in the world." And, Sylbert knew, it was not his movies that had catapulted Polanski to this notoriety, at least not completely. The murders on Cielo Drive had been the catalyst. Like the victims of the crime, Polanski had been infected by it, and he felt like a "freak."

Seeking quiet, he now flew to London, but the press was full of the killings—and Polanski. He returned to California, moving into Richard Sylbert's Malibu beach house. Sylbert found him distraught. Trying to console him, he reassured Polanski that he was tougher than most people. "Yeah," replied Polanski, "but who wants to be tougher?" Polanski told Sylbert that when he had put Sharon on the boat, he had felt he might never see her again. "Whenever I get happy," Polanski said, "I always have a terrible feeling." To Christine Larene, Polanski even spoke of suicide.

Someone had to deal with the practical matters of Sharon's estate, but whenever his agent, Bill Tennant, would bring up the subject, Polanski would only respond: "Give it away. I don't want it. I wish I had spent more. I wish there had been more dresses. . . ." Polanski was too distraught to have any interest in the dispersal of Sharon's remaining possessions. When Tennant protested that he had to think of the future, Polanski's reply was simple and bitter: "Bill, what can they do to me? I've already been poor."

In December 1969, after four months of investigation, the case broke. Susan Atkins, one of the girls who had joined Charles Manson's "family," and who was in jail for another crime, confessed to a cellmate. With Atkins' confession and the arrest of Charles Manson and several other "family" members, it became clear that Sharon Tate and the others had been chosen at random. Manson had ordered his followers to go to the house once rented by Terry Melcher. The evidence indicates that Manson was aware that Melcher was no longer living on Cielo Drive. He only wanted to kill "whoever" was there. It was also members of the Manson "family" who were responsible for the LaBianca murders.

On August 9, Charles "Tex" Watson, twenty-three, Susan Atkins, twenty-one, Patricia Krenwinkel, twenty-one, and Linda Kasabian, twenty (Kasabian was never prosecuted in return for becoming a witness for the prosecution), drove off into the darkness, over the freeways and back roads, in the direction of Benedict Canyon and Cielo Drive. Manson directed their moves without leaving the Spahn Movie Ranch, formerly rented as a set for westerns, where the "family" lived. Asleep on the couch, Wojtek Frykowski was awakened by the intruders standing over him. Even half-awake, debilitated by drugs, the powerful Frykowski put up a fight. His ravaged body testified to the monumental struggle he had waged for his life.

Once they had hold of Frykowski, they brought the others into the living room. Jay Sebring was the first of the four to die. He objected to the intruders' treatment of Sharon and tried to appeal to their compassion, reminding them that Sharon was pregnant. In response, Watson shot Sebring. Sharon Tate begged for her and her baby's lives. Gibby Folger offered money and credit cards and managed to escape out the back door—to be caught and slaughtered. Frykowski kept fighting, even with multiple stab wounds rapidly draining the blood from his veins.

While Manson's capture refueled the public obsession

with details about the victims as well as the murderers, Polanski felt that the case was closed for him, and he decided to try to forget as much as he could. The public, however, wouldn't forget. Best-selling accounts by Manson's prosecutor Vincent Bugliosi, and hippie poet Ed Sanders, as well as exploitation books, recapitulated the gory details. Finally, Jerzy Kosinski wrote a novel, *Blind Date*, in which the slaughter was meticulously fantasized, using an arsenal of fictive techniques. Driven by a compulsion to repeat, writers and readers re-enacted the killings countless times in their imagination.

eleven

THE MURDERERS CAUGHT, Polanski fled Los Angeles for Switzerland. He told Victor Lownes that he wanted to escape the public eye. Having scrapped *The Day of the Dolphin* project (for lack of concentration), he sought to lose himself in skiing and sex—temporarily forgetting about work. The tragedy made everything appear futile, pointless. No project seemed right. Polanski and Bill Tennant were aware that his next film had to be carefully chosen. *Roman Polanski* couldn't direct just *anything*—for whatever he did would be received in terms of the crime that had infected him. Polanski was no longer making films to create an image. From this point on, his films would respond to an image he no longer fully controlled. Obviously, he couldn't return to his earlier project about cannibalism. He decided to adapt and film the best-selling *Papillon* and instructed Tennant to set up a deal. But Tennant found producer Robert Dorfman and distributor Walter Reade, who owned film rights to the book, unable to put up the kind of money Polanski needed.

Rebuffed on *Papillon*, Polanski wanted something quickly. He contacted his friend Kenneth Tynan, literary adviser to the National Theatre in London, and proposed collaborating on a film based on *Macbeth*. They would write a screenplay together, and Tynan would continue as adviser during shooting. Polanski had been interested in Shakespeare since childhood when he pasted a still from Laurence Olivier's *Hamlet* on the wall of his room and saw the film innumerable times. Polanski had toyed with the idea of adapting Shakespeare before but feared no one would back him. Now, convinced that nothing was "worthwhile," Polanski was drawn to the coherent delineation of character in *Macbeth*, a play he had never seen on stage. Knowing that the best films, or those he liked best—like

116

Citizen Kane—focus on character, Polanski decided that this emphasis in *Macbeth* made it well suited for adaptation.

Polanski had met Tynan when working on *Repulsion*. Hoping to do a stage production at the National Theatre, Polanski had approached Tynan—but no deal was made. At first Tynan was uncomfortable with Polanski, who, he felt, "didn't move in an upper class world." But Polanski worked on cultivating him. Tynan decided that although Polanski socialized with "studs and toughs"—"any man who lived a dangerous life"—he also desired friendship with intellectuals. Uneasy about the milieu of soft-core pornographers in which Polanski operated, Tynan was no prude—just contemptuous of people he dismissed as sleazy. When in 1969 he organized his notorious erotic revue, *Oh! Calcutta!*, Tynan negotiated with Polanski for two four-minute films, each a single take. Tynan conceived of *Oh! Calcutta!* as porn for the thinking man, and Polanski decided to shoot two studies of voyeurism, along the lines of *Toothy Smile*, unknown in the West. For the first act, Polanski proposed a shot through a window. The voyeur would be invisible throughout—like the camera. A girl would appear and strip, but her breasts, buttocks and crotch would be obscured by a clever arrangement of furniture, bric-a-brac and wind-blown curtains. Another girl would appear, strip and make love to her friend—the specifics of their sex-play remaining invisible. Finally one girl would reach orgasm—but why we could only guess. For the frustrated voyeur, the forbidden isn't quite off screen or between shots. Like Polanski's solution to the problem of the demon-child in *Rosemary's Baby*, this film idea explored ironic possibilities for simultaneously exposing and concealing on screen.

A static camera and an invisible, frustrated voyeur also figured in the short for the second act. This time the view would be into a train window, beside which a girl is seated. A man would enter her compartment and sit opposite her. The girl's expression would reveal that he had exposed himself, although we wouldn't actually see the act. Next she would lift her skirt—but this too was to be cut off, merely suggested. They would begin to copulate—and when someone passes in the corridor behind them, they dive beneath the window frame, where we can't see. Delighted by Polanski's concepts, Tynan called them "cock-teasing films"—perfect intellectual porn. But they remained unmade. Polanski insisted on working with a wide screen, beyond the initial limited budget of *Oh! Calcutta!*.

When Polanski proposed the *Macbeth* script, Tynan was curious. Although unrealized, Polanski's ideas for the *Oh! Calcutta!* films had intrigued him. Also, Tynan had long admired *Knife in the Water*, which he deemed "extremely adult." More recently, *Rosemary's Baby* had hit him "at a very deep level." Disturbed by the film, he had found it "surprisingly understated, considering what the subject was." In spite of Polanski's denials, Tynan suspected that he believed in evil as a force in the world. Tynan thought *Rosemary's Baby* "one of the very few films that made one consider the possibility that there was any such thing as absolute evil."

Tynan was the perfect collaborator, sensitive to Polanski's emotional state. Tynan had known Sharon and saw that Polanski had come "to rely on her emotionally more than he expected he would." Before beginning work, the collaborators agreed not to discuss the recent tragedy. They also avoided talking politics. Espousing increasingly right-wing views, Polanski was intolerant of Tynan's leftist sympathies.

The two men spent six intensive weeks in the study of Polanski's London home, scouring the play for cinematic possibilities. As he had done with Jerzy Skolimowski on *Knife in the Water*, Polanski acted out the roles with Tynan. Working on Duncan's murder, the shirtless pair tumbled on the bed and the floor. Exchanging roles, they tried it several times—each slightly different—until, finally, Tynan realized that they were being watched through the window by a staid group of neighbors who thought them "a pair of sadomasochistic queers."

While working, Polanski and Tynan weren't always alone in the house. Girls would often lounge in the living room, leafing through magazines or listening to music while waiting for Polanski. Meanwhile, the collaborators cut parts of the play and visually amplified others. Wherever possible, words were realized in concrete cinematic images. Tynan was amazed at Polanski's command of textual matters, his knowledge of the play and its possibilities. Polanski's usual screenwriting approach is to indicate dialogue and action but not to spell out camera movement or choreography, leaving most of these decisions for later. At the close of a day's work, Tynan would type what they had done. Polanski sought "to turn into images those parts of the play which are obviously related to action, but which would be restricted on stage by technical limitations."

Tynan thought *Macbeth* the most supernatural of Shakespearean plays—apart from *The Tempest*—and wanted to make its occult elements as realistic as possible, to appeal to a contemporary audience. For instance, it was important to him that Macbeth actually drink the witches' potion—something he had never seen done on stage. In Tynan's version, what Macbeth sees—usually seen by the witches too—is a subjective point of view, a drugged hallucination. But Tynan also sought to show a world *beyond* the character and his intrigues, a lesson Tynan had learned from the Soviet director Grigori Kozintsev's *Hamlet*, which both he and Polanski admired.

While Polanski and Tynan labored on the scenario, Bill Tennant sought financing. But Polanski had been right: no one wanted to bankroll a Shakespearean film—even though the director was now a proven commercial success. Rebuffed everywhere, Tennant talked to Victor Lownes about the idea of getting backing from Playboy. The timing was right: Playboy was about to open a film division and wanted a "prestige" film for its first project. *Macbeth* had several things going for it. Tynan was a *Playboy* contributing editor and had written high-brow pieces for the magazine. Polanski was arty, commercial and Lownes's close friend. Finally, what could be more prestigious than Shakespeare? Lownes went to bat for Polanski, endorsing the project to Hugh Hefner. Tennant flew to London to talk money to Hefner—and, in the Hilton Hotel, in Marbella, Spain, a deal was consummated—for a $2.4 million budget.

Observing from a distance, Michael Klinger, producer on *Repulsion* and *Cul de Sac*, predicted trouble. As Polanski's buddy, Lownes wouldn't be able to control him as a disinterested businessman could. Polanski, Klinger knew, worked best with the pressure of someone monitoring him and his excesses. Playboy backing posed another problem: from the start it was rumored that the film's use of nudity was to please its backers. Also, the blend of witchcraft and eroticism—actually, a traditional approach—was to be often ascribed to Playboy influence. Playboy, however, kept hands off throughout—giving Polanski and Tynan total artistic liberty. Too much, thought Klinger.

Polanski and Andrew Braunsberg formed a production company called Caliban Films, after the monstrous offspring of the devil's union with a witch in Shakespeare's *The Tempest*. A completion guarantee was secured for the expensive project. If Polanski went over budget, the film's completion was assured, but in that case, producers and director would be at the mercy of the guaranteeing company. Even if Polanski were retained, he would lose his equity in the film. In every way, it was in Polanski's interest to remain within the budget agreed upon with Hefner.

The script completed, Polanski had to decide upon actors. He and Tynan wanted to cast young people as Macbeth and his wife, instead of what Tynan called the usual "sixty-year-olds and menopausals." Youth, they felt, added plausibility to the theme of ambition. Being inexperienced, with their lives ahead of them, a young Macbeth and Lady Macbeth would have much at stake in their manipulations, and the drama would acquire new resonance. "I see Macbeth as a young, open-faced warrior," said Polanski, "who is gradually sucked into a whirlpool of events because of his ambition. When he meets the weird sisters and hears their prophecy, he's like the man who hopes to win a million—a gambler for high stakes." Polanski and Tynan sought to emphasize a conflict between age and usurping youth that would make the film of interest to a young audience. They were convinced that if young, Macbeth and Lady Macbeth would be more sympathetic characters in general. Most important for the scenarists was the added erotic angle, for Polanski was intent on developing the "sexual thing between the Macbeths." "How could any man be influenced by a nag?" asked Polanski, "He'd say, 'Shut your trap, my dearest love, thou borest me to death.'"

As in *Knife in the Water* and *Cul de Sac*, Polanski was interested in the female's tactics of humiliation and manipulation. Lured by a sexually appealing woman, Macbeth would be driven to prove what Tynan called his "machismo." Tynan decided that there was no textual reason for following the tradition of casting older actors, who usually played the roles only because they were senior in the theatrical companies and in line for the meatiest parts.

As first choice, Polanski sought Albert Finney for Macbeth, but Finney responded that he would act the part only in a film he directed himself. When Nicol Williamson was mentioned, Polanski said, "This man has got to be sexually attractive, and Williamson isn't." He also told Tynan he found Williamson "vocally monotonous." Polanski and Tynan didn't want an awesome Shakespearean performance from their Macbeth and insisted that the lines be spoken almost as natural speech.

Tynan's reason was his desire for a realistic approach to the material. He suspected that Polanski was insecure about the idea of working with anyone strongly identified as a Shakespearean actor, for he wanted to be able to dominate whomever was chosen. Tynan's suspicion was confirmed during production when he noticed that Polanski avoided giving line readings because these were English actors—even if they weren't strict Shakespeareans—and Polanski seemed uncomfortable about giving them his interpretation of Shakespeare.

Flying back to London after a visit to Paris, Polanski met the handsome twenty-eight-year-old actor, Jon Finch, whose face he had seen in a casting directory. Finch had appeared on an English TV series named "Counterstrike" and had recently played a homosexual in John Schlesinger's *Sunday, Bloody Sunday*. Impressed by Finch's looks and manner, Polanski invited him for an all-night session with Tynan. When they got to London, at about 9 P.M., Polanski called Tynan and told him about Finch. Tynan met them at Polanski's, and Finch read from the part for hours, while Polanski video-taped. By noon the next day, when they had finished, Polanski decided this was the Macbeth he had been looking for. Later he would even tell *The New York Times* that he had "invented" Jon Finch.

During shooting, others noticed Polanski's tendency to play with Finch. There was one scene in which Finch takes a log, tosses it into a fire, then starts to speak. The scene was discussed, and Finch went to have his makeup adjusted. While he was gone, Polanski had propmen nail down the log. The actor returned, Polanski yelled, "All right, action!" and Finch reached for the log, which wouldn't budge.

As his Lady Macbeth, Polanski cast twenty-five-year-old Francesca Annis. She had played Ophelia in Nicol Williamson's *Hamlet* in New York and had appeared as a handmaiden in *Cleopatra*. Polanski wasn't happy with the actresses he was interviewing. But when Annis read her lines—Tynan observed, "like a little girl"—Polanski was charmed. This childish quality would be the means by which Polanski's Lady Macbeth would manipulate her husband.

Reviewing the film, *The London Observer* would describe Annis as "a vulnerable troubled child" possessing a "nymphetish quality." Like Mia Farrow in *Rosemary's Baby* or Nastassia Kinski in *Tess,* she is a Polanski fantasy female. The result was a distinctly Polanskian—and decidedly eccentric—variant on one of the most powerful female characters ever created in English literature. "I thought Lady Macbeth should have been older," Annis told *The New York Times*, "but Roman didn't have to do much arm twisting to persuade me!" As an actress, she was—as one of her past acting coaches observed during shooting— "available" to Polanski, ready to heed his directions. Polanski even used the drug amyl nitrite to stimulate her before acting, crushing a capsule beneath her nostrils. Because she was so malleable, permitting Polanski to shape her role as he wished, her former coach felt her performance lacked the tension that enlivens the best performances Polanski is capable of getting.

Polanski and Tynan decided to spice up Lady Macbeth's sleepwalking scene by having her nude. (Because Annis was self-conscious about being nude, Polanski discreetly cleared the set.) Tynan claimed that the justification for the nudity was that there were no nightgowns in Macbeth's time. But this was a spurious rationalization since Lady

Macbeth would probably have slept in her undergarments. Thus the nudity in Polanski's sleepwalking scene was of doubtful authenticity.

Extensive location shooting was necessary on *Macbeth,* and Polanski and Braunsberg embarked on a quest for the right places, finally choosing Wales and Northumberland. In Wales, four grueling weeks of tempestuous weather were endured by a crew of 170 in Snowdonia National Park. Shooting began with an accident.

The opening witches' scene was shot in a remote spot in the mountains. To get to the location, the three were driven for two miles in a Land-Rover, along roads left behind by the Romans. Beyond this, assistants carried the women to a battered building where Polanski and crew awaited. Howling winds and pounding rains made shooting almost impossible. The cameraman was blown off a boom and tumbled into a crevice—narrowly escaping death.

The unanticipated weather made Polanski's job hell. His barked instructions were almost inaudible, visibility was poor, and subtleties of performance were lost in the gale. Cast and crew struggled to keep themselves going with vitamin-C tablets. Told that Hugh Hefner's birthday was near, Polanski decided to make a gift on film: a group of naked hags singing "Happy Birthday, Dear Hef," which he dispatched to his benefactor in the Playboy mansion.

For two weeks Polanski and company worked in castles he and Braunsberg discovered in Northumberland and on nearby Holy Island, where he'd shot *Cul de Sac.* Polanski and Tynan hoped to develop a strong visual contrast between the castles Macbeth inhabits before and after he becomes king. For the first, Lindisfarne Castle on Holy Island was selected; for the second, Bamburgh Castle in Northumberland. The film completed, Tynan would feel that the intended contrast had failed, the two castles blurring into each other. Working on location on a grand scale, Polanski would complain that he preferred the studio, where he could focus on character rather than the sweeping backdrops to the action.

The remainder of the twenty-five weeks of shooting were accomplished at Shepperton Studios, where production designer Wilfrid Shingleton painstakingly constructed interiors and exteriors to capture the authentic feel of the time. Consciously copying Kozintsev's *Hamlet,* Polanski and Tynan used domestic animals to suggest life beyond Macbeth's personal drama. Polanski's directorial tasks included activating and choreographing chickens, geese, doves and dogs. Demanding precision, he was frequently exasperated in his attempts to get the animals to behave exactly the way he wanted.

One day, Polanski was directing a courtyard scene on a sound stage. In the scene a cart arrives amid the general bustle and cacophony of animals and people—all drenched by a sudden downpour. Polanski explained precisely how he envisioned the action, how the rain was to begin just before the cart entered. Each movement—whether of people, beasts or cart—was to begin at a specific time in relation to other action. But so many pictorial elements were involved that the scene virtually defied direction. Sprinklers drenched the set with mock rain at the wrong times, and two or three hours would be needed for drying off. Frustrated by the delays, Polanski realized that he had to simplify the take. "We'll do the whole thing with me directing on a bull-horn—without sound," he announced. "We can dub in the sound afterwards."

This time, the people, the animals, the things were all in place exactly as Polanski had indicated—and the action began. "OK, let the dogs go!" he called. "People moving! Chickens! Get those fucking chickens moving! OK, rain! Rain! OK, cut! Cut!" Shooting stopped. Furious, Polanski jumped up and down. "What'd you do?" he shrieked. "You said 'Cut!' Roman," replied the assistant director. "You ruined my fucking picture!" Polanski shouted. "But, Roman, you said, 'Cut!' " "No, no, I said, 'Cut!' Bring in the 'cut'!" "You mean 'cart.' " "That's right," Polanski said, "the 'cut'!"

With his practiced eye, Polanski was aware when the slightest detail of a scene struck a wrong note. Typically with him, each scene was shot numerous times, on expensive color film. One morning, working on a complex tableau in a castle interior, Polanski seemed inordinately perplexed—but no one dared ask why. They had been shooting the tableau for hours, but Polanski still wasn't satisfied.

Usually animated, he stared intently at the set, as if scanning the crowded composition for something he had not yet identified, paying scant attention to suggestions that they shoot the scene once more before lunch. "No, no, it's wrong, it's wrong!" Polanski muttered. When they heard him, the crew backed away, sensing that he might fly into a rage any second. Another five minutes passed—in silence. "Excuse me, Roman . . . can we, uh . . . we've got everybody in position now . . ." "No!" shouted Polanski, walking off the set. It was understood that the others were to wait where they were. Fifteen minutes later he returned hauling an enormous sack. In moments, two propmen were piling ashes beneath the braziers that were part of the scene and were supposed to have been burning all night. Without ashes below them, the tableau would have been incomplete—the kind of fault that disturbs a director like Polanski.

Polanski thought nothing of spending three hours to get a candle to flicker properly. As an added touch to a sloppy banquet table, Polanski stuffed hunks of bread into his mouth, chewed heartily, then spat the bread onto the table. Having observed the filming of a lengthy fight sequence—crammed with raucous action—Polanski had isolated small details in the opening moments that needed polishing. Dissatisfied with an actor who needed to look grubbier, Polanski hurled mud in his face—a gesture some took as emblematic of his attitude toward actors. To Tynan, Polanski spoke of the actors as "comics" and "monkeys."

Polanski is a director who seeks to create a performance for the actor—rather than permit him his own interpretation. Even with the smallest roles, Polanski was careful to exercise complete control. For one minor insert, an actor was asked to sip a drink, then look up at Macbeth. Polanski set up the shot and yelled, "Action!" But when the actor reached for the cup and drank, Polanski yelled, "Cut!" The actor couldn't understand what was wrong. "Why do you do *this thing* with the cup?" asked Polanski, aping the way the actor had sipped from the cup. Puzzled, the actor replied, "I was trying to—" But he couldn't complete his thought. "Just drink from the cup this time," Polanski instructed him. But as soon as they resumed, Polanski again cried, "Cut!" "The way you drink is good," Polanski reassured the actor. "But the way you look up—why do you do *that?*" "Well," the actor replied, "I was acting—trying to give it some importance." "Leave that to me," said Polanski. "You just drink from the cup, that's all." For Polanski, it is the director who bestows importance—not the actor.

Polanski and Tynan were eager to include a bear-baiting sequence in their film but had trouble locating a proper bear. The first was too gentle, cringing at the sight of the ferocious dogs it was to fight, so another was acquired. This second was a killer. Walking past the cage, a crew member was pawed by the beast, who attempted to haul the man inside. "Stop playing with the fucking bear!" shouted Polanski. But even he finally realized the hazard the bear posed and decided to use a stunt man, named Reg, in a bear suit. For his confrontation with the dogs, Reg placed metal plates in the suit's arms to protect himself from being bitten. But hearing the dogs snarling and leaping at passersby, he grew edgy.

When Reg came into the studio, he found Polanski waiting. At the sight of the bear-suited man, the dogs went wild, growling and baring their teeth, frenziedly pawing the slippery floors. Nervously, Reg asked Polanski to run through the stunt first with a single dog. The moment the beast was let off its chain, it lunged into Reg's arm with such ferocity that Reg told Polanski he could not possibly handle the original three dogs planned for the shot. Polanski leaned over to the dogs' handler so that Reg wouldn't hear him. "We let three dogs go," he instructed the handler. "If it doesn't work, we cut the scene."

Meanwhile, the shot was set up, with a fiber glass collar attached to Reg's neck and tied to the base of a pillar with a four-foot chain. Then the bear's head was slipped onto Reg so that he could see out through the neck. Everything was ready.

"Action!" yelled Polanski, and the handler let the three dogs go. One went for Reg's leg, another for his arm, and the third for his crotch. Reg went straight up the pillar. "Get 'em off, Roman! Get 'em off!"

"Keep your head down, Reg!" Polanski shouted. "We can see your face!"

Finally Polanski decided that the bear-baiting sequence was more trouble than it was worth. In the completed film, the tearing apart of the bear takes place off screen—"mercifully," wrote Pauline Kael. But Polanski wasn't being merciful: he just couldn't figure out how to show it.

By January, *Macbeth* was over budget and behind schedule. Tynan felt the trouble began with the weather problems in Wales. More basically, however, Polanski had become a director who spared no expense—a far cry from his early low-budget days. Threatened under the completion guarantee, Polanski refused to economize or speed up —a strategy he had used with Paramount on *Rosemary's Baby*. Under the completion guarantee, Polanski and Braunsberg would be bumped as producers—with Polanski's position as director in serious question. But Polanski reacted indifferently, taking off for a ski weekend in a helicopter just when pressures were reaching a peak. The money men who had issued the completion guarantee turned up on the set with an ultimatum to rush shooting— or else. By now Polanski had lost his equity but was still cool—proceeding as usual. The situation was an embarrassment for Lownes, who had promoted Polanski in the first place. He perceived that Polanski was "playing child" with him now—even offering to quit voluntarily when he knew Lownes would never accept such a move. Finally, Hugh Hefner stepped in and saved Polanski by offering to put up the extra money himself. The guarantors, however, refused to cancel the original fee they had charged—even though the guarantee was being terminated. "OK, keep the money," Hefner told them, "but don't destroy my film." This gallantry lost Hefner money on both ends—but Polanski was Lownes's friend. Tennant thought Hefner "a real *mensch*" for coming through like this. Thereafter, Hefner put no pressure on Polanski, saying only, "Make it as fast and as well as you can." And to top everything, he gave Polanski back his equity. In the end, the two-hour nineteen-minute *Macbeth* would go ten weeks over schedule and $600,000 over budget.

With *Macbeth* about to open, Polanski gave an interview to the London *Evening Standard*'s Stanley Edwards. Originally scheduled for a London restaurant called

L'Ambassadeur, the interview was shifted to the Playboy Club's VIP Room. Playboy Productions sought maximum publicity for its investment. Edwards reported that Polanski spoke "with a candor that was surprising considering Mr. Hugh Hefner's Playboy Enterprises put up the money for his new film." "I don't really like it here," Polanski told Edwards, referring to the Playboy Club. When trout was served, Polanski sent it back as inedible—surely not a good publicity move for his benefactor. Edwards inquired about the Playboy financing. *"Pecunia non olet,"* Polanski replied ["Money doesn't smell"]. "Someone has to put money into the film industry," he said. "Why then not Mr. Hefner?"

When the interview appeared, Lownes was stunned. It wasn't just bad business; friendship was involved. Hefner had backed *Macbeth*—and saved Polanski midway—largely as a favor to Lownes, whose judgment he respected. Feeling that he had been used, Lownes telephoned Polanski, who hung up on his complaints. When they met at the film's gala opening on February 2 at the Plaza Theatre in Piccadilly Circus, relations were cool. A benefit for the Association of Spina Bifida and Hydrocephalus, it was attended by assorted Playboy bunnies as well as Princess Anne representing the Royal Family. "I'll never make another film with horses in it," quipped Polanski as he came face to face with the princess when Lownes introduced them. Polanski and Lownes never spoke again. The friendship ended in a way that confused Lownes, who wrote an embarrassed letter to Hefner on February 24.

In the letter, Lownes told Hefner that he and Polanski were no longer in contact and there was now no way he could get him to promote the film. Lownes had discussed Polanski's behavior with others who knew him well, and he reported their explanations to Hefner. "Gene Gutowski analyses Roman's attitude as being the result of his 'not having anything more that he can get out of you and Playboy.'" Andrew Braunsberg had apparently been less gentle: "When I asked Andy Braunsberg why Roman had at the least not attempted to explain or apologise for the outburst [the statements he had made to the *Evening Standard*], he assured me that Roman does not feel that he has done anything wrong, and when I remonstrated that friends don't talk about each other in that way, especially to the press, he said, 'Well, maybe he's not your friend, he's your enemy.' "

Lownes confessed, "The thing that is so distressing to me is that for years I did everything I possibly could to be helpful to this son-of-a-bitch, and had only recently come round to realise that I was merely being exploited by him. . . . The thing that bugs me is that I dragged everybody else into this mess, almost as if I had a blind spot where Roman is concerned." He concluded by telling Hefner how much he appreciated his not having "scored" him for "bad judgement and the unfortunate consequences that this has had for Playboy. The fact that you don't proves to me, as always, that you are my very best friend."

Responding to Lownes, Hefner spoke of Polanski with distance and admirable compassion. Polanski had violated the principles of friendship valued by the Playboy philosophy, and Hefner seriously attempted to explain why. Saddened by Polanski's behavior, Hefner thought him insecure, self-destructive and incapable of sustaining a close relationship. Talent and success were no excuse for the shabby treatment of a close friend like Lownes.

Lownes took one parting shot at Polanski. Some years before, while he and Sharon were abroad, Polanski had a "solid gold prick" sculpted for Lownes as a surprise gift. Polanski concealed the object in his trousers to get through British customs. Now Lownes decided to put the prick in a box and return it to Polanski. "In view of recent developments," read the enclosed card, "I no longer care to have this full-length, life-size portrait of you around the house. I'm sure you'll have no difficulty finding some 'friend' you can shove it up."

Polanski's relations with the press were also stormy—his resentment lingering of the media coverage of the Manson murders. "What happened was reviewed in terms of my films," Polanski complained in *The New York Times*. "Now it's vice versa. Now my films are reviewed in terms of what happened. If I did a comedy, aha!—it would not be right. If I did a murder, aha!" With *Macbeth*, Polanski had done a murder. Reviewing it, when it opened at the Playboy

Theater in New York, *Newsweek*'s Paul D. Zimmerman wrote that "parallels between the Manson murders (which took Polanski's wife Sharon Tate) and the mad, bloody acts of these beautiful, lost Macbeths keep pressing themselves on the viewer—as though Shakespeare's play has provided Polanski with some strange opportunity to act out his own complicated feelings about Satanism, mystic ties, blood, evil and revenge." In the Chicago *Sun-Times*, Roger Ebert wrote: "It is impossible to watch a film directed by Roman Polanski and not react on more than one level to such images as a baby being 'untimely ripped from his mother's womb.' " For Ebert, "Polanski's characters resemble Manson. They are anti-intellectual, witless and driven by deep, shameful wells of lust and violence." Instead of discovering sources of Polanski's film in the Manson murders, *Women's Wear Daily* critic Gail Rock complained that "it is an assault on the audience that seems to me to divert us from the intellectual thrust of *Macbeth* and turns us into voyeurs at a killing spree that makes Manson and his friends pale in comparison." Perversely, for *Women's Wear Daily*, Polanski seemed to have gone one better than the Mansons. In the most sensitive of the reviews, Pauline Kael, in *The New Yorker*, thoroughly—and forcefully—articulated a critical problem posed by the film: "In the Manson case, there was an eerie element that the public responded to. Even though we knew that Roman Polanski had nothing whatever to do with causing the murder of his wife and unborn child and friends, the massacre seemed a vision realized from his nightmare movies. And there was an element of guilt and embarrassment in this connection we made." Polanski, Kael noted, "didn't quite understand that this connection was inevitable." Her tactful admission of earlier embarrassment permitted Kael to confront head-on Polanski's complaint about those who would review his films in terms of the killings. In Polanski's statement, Kael detected "either a strange form of naivete or a divided consciousness." Casting aside all squeamishness about intentionality, Kael wrote: "One sees the Manson murders in this 'Macbeth' because the director has put them there."

In the unrealized shorts for *Oh! Calcutta!*, Polanski had hoped to explore the use of the tension between on-screen and off-screen space: the sexual acts would remain unseen, though hinted at within the frame. On the contrary, in his *Macbeth*, violence generally unseen in more typical Shakespearean productions is shown in gory detail. "You have to show violence the way it is," Polanski told *The New York Times*. "If you don't show it realistically, then that's immoral and harmful. If you don't upset people, then that's obscenity." Wherever possible, Polanski sketched in the violence only described in the text. In this, Polanski explicitly followed Polish critic Jan Kott's interpretation of *Macbeth*: "Blood, in *Macbeth*," wrote Kott in *Shakespeare Our Contemporary*, "is not just a metaphor. It leaves its stains on hands and faces, on daggers and swords. . . . A production of *Macbeth* not evoking a picture of the world flooded with blood, would inevitably be false." This picture is strongly evoked in Polanski's version—too strongly for some tastes. Gordon Gow wrote in *Films and Filming:* "There is plenty of blood in it, of course. One of the killings reminded me vividly of what happened when a sharp knife was applied to the throat of a pig during an educational tour of a slaughterhouse which I was obliged to take in younger and unhappier days."

Not surprisingly, the murder of sweet, innocent Lady Macduff and her children—assaulted while Macduff is away—is highlighted in Polanski's version. Smearing mock blood on a child actress for this scene, Polanski discovered that her name was Sharon. And because of their obvious resonance for Polanski, there was tension on the set when Macduff's poignant words on the killings were delivered. As Macduff, Terence Bayler differed with the director on a fine point of interpretation. "No," concluded Polanski when he wished to argue no longer, "you'll do it this way. *I know*."

One of the film's more shocking effects is Macbeth's decapitation. A false head was attached to a full-size suit of armor, the arms and legs of which were manipulated by a child within. Stuck on a pike, the severed head was exhibited by Polanski himself. "I don't know that you can speak of shock," Polanski insisted. "I don't really know what is shocking. When you tell the story of a man who is beheaded, you have to show how they cut off his head. If you don't, it's like telling a dirty joke and leaving out the punch line."

The obvious predilection for brutal detail led critics to wonder about Polanski. During shooting, Polanski had complained to *Time* that he was now more famous as Sharon Tate's widower than as a director. "It's ridiculous," he lamented, "but because of the association, there's a feeling that whatever I come up with here will be quite grotesque." But the completed film fulfilled the predictions he had scornfully denied—a contradictory impulse typical of Polanski.

"All that is good here," wrote *Newsweek*, "seems but a pretext for close-ups of knives drawing geysers of blood from the flesh of men, women and children. No chance to revel in gore is passed up. We watch bodies crushed and mutilated by spiked clubs, limbs severed, hands bathed in crimson, necks broken, heads lopped off. . . . Is the decapitation of Macbeth and the parading of his head on a spear an indispensable reality? If so, then *Macbeth* is a work of art—in the grand manner of Buchenwald, Lidice and, yes, the Manson murders." Polanski was being equated with Manson again—but also with Hitler: the critic blurring crucial distinctions between imagination and reality.

Like the best-selling books on the Manson killings, *Macbeth* was an imaginative repetition of simultaneously repugnant and fascinating events. If the public was permitted its endless nightmare visions of the scene, why not Polanski? Still, *Macbeth* got the better of him. (The most wounding criticism of all came from the Polish filmmaker Jerzy Kawalerowicz, who found Polanski's *Macbeth* curious for what it revealed about the dangers of overreaching oneself.) Polanski had turned to the comfort of the classic for its appealing order, its emphasis on character, and its mythification of private experience. But working on a grand scale to which he was unaccustomed, he failed to come up with the proper visual style for his film. As Polanski understood so well in *Repulsion*, cinema must show, not tell. Now, much as he had marshalled the enormous production resources at his disposal, this *Macbeth* hadn't crystallized. The greatest Shakespearean films—such as Kozintsev's *Hamlet* or Kurosawa's *Throne of Blood* [*Macbeth*]—are commanding in their pictorial compositions, their visual interpretations of the literary text, in ways that Polanski's is not. Ironically, for all the talk of showing *everything*, in Polanski's *Macbeth* the fascination is off screen, in the director's personal drama.

twelve

SINCE ADOLESCENCE, Polanski had been a devoted body builder. If he couldn't be tall and handsome like Frykowski or Skolimowski, he would at least be able to do fifty deep knee bends on a single leg—a skill he worked at for years. "I've got to be physically fit to survive," Polanski confided to Kenneth Tynan, discussing the plight of small people. Anxious to be able to defend himself, Polanski studied martial arts with kung-fu exponent Bruce Lee—like him, compact but sinewy. Mesmerized by machismo, Polanski was drawn to active men who took risks. With Jay Sebring he had shared a passion for sports cars and high speeds and in London had cultivated the friendship of daredevil racing driver Jackie Stewart. Still editing *Macbeth*, Polanski took a weekend off to produce a documentary about Stewart at the Monte Carlo Grand Prix, *Weekend of Champions*. To Victor Lownes's horror, when *Macbeth* opened, Polanski devoted his time to promoting the documentary instead, which had cost about £25,000 to make. "Naturally," Lownes reported to Hefner, "he would rather forget about the $3,000,000 disaster and concentrate on this."

Macbeth completed, Tynan and Polanski went to Saint-Tropez to discuss another project. Polanski wanted to make a full-length feature in only nine long shots—a startling idea, because ninety-minute films can run from six hundred to one thousand shots, even more. Hitchcock had experimented in this way in *Rope*, with its extraordinary ten-minute shots. The story Polanski had in mind involved nine of a man's erotic relationships. One shot would be devoted to a day in each entanglement. Requiring only nine takes—and nine days to shoot—the film would be remarkably cheap to make. But for Polanski, its real interest lay elsewhere: the man would be based on the late actor Zbigniew Cybulski, the so-called "Polish James Dean." Like Dean in

America, Cybulski was a mythicized figure in postwar Poland, his erotic mystique enhanced by his untimely death when crushed while trying to leap onto a moving train. Tynan saw that Polanski "worshiped" Cybulski because of his intense sexuality and extreme life-style. Like *Weekend of Champions*, the Cybulski film would be an homage to a macho ideal—all the more meaningful for Cybulski's associations with Poland and its dominant director, Andrzej Wajda, whose *Ashes and Diamonds* had spawned the Cybulski myth.

Discussion of the Cybulski film didn't go beyond the intoxicating Saint-Tropez weekend. Polanski decided to collaborate again with Brach, who had a vague idea for a script set in winter. But when they talked to Carlo Ponti, the Italian producer, the latter said he would be more interested in a summer film and invited them to work at his villa near Amalfi, Italy. Entirely secluded, the sprawling Mediterranean villa was reached by a cable car shaped like a bird cage, which gave Polanski a story idea: arriving at the villa in the bird cage, an innocent young girl discovers situations beyond her comprehension. Not even the inhabitants of the pale white villa understand anything that is happening. Along with his penchant for blood and violence, Polanski also has a nonsensical streak—drawing on the tradition of Polish absurdist writers like Gombrowicz and Witkiewicz, and encouraged by Brach's French surrealist nuttiness. "My films are the expression of momentary desires," Polanski told *Le Monde* in 1972. "I follow my instincts, but in a disciplined way." True—but to varying degrees. Sometimes, there's more instinct; sometimes, more discipline.

Two months after his idea in the bird cage, Polanski was shooting on location at Ponti's villa and in a studio in Rome, with Andrew Braunsberg as executive producer.

The result, *What?*, was a turnabout from the classical structure of *Macbeth*—with the latter's well-defined beginning, middle and end. Instead, *What?* was structured entirely on "momentary desires." That is, more on "instincts," less on "discipline." Events proceed without conventional motivation, as in free association—or plotless pornographic films. The bird cage deposits the ethereal, nymphetish heroine at the villa, and, as in novels by Sade, the villa's enclosure frees the action from the constraints of an external, now distant world. After *Macbeth*, Polanski went slumming, letting his thoughts—and story—wander. Without a classical narrative armature, *What?* is unadulterated "Polanski"—a crazy quilt of libidinous scenes. Despite his purported concern with character, there aren't any here—just interchangeable parts in soft-core sexual scenarios. The reciprocity between victim and victimizer—a favorite Polanski motif since *The Fat and the Lean*—has Nancy (Sydne Rome) lashing Alex (Marcello Mastroianni) in one scene, then him lashing her in another. Without three-dimensional characters, the play of power and humiliation is more important than who does what to whom, or when.

Polanski's female lead, Sydne Rome, had come to Italy from America to try out for *Candy*. She was still living there when she was cast for *What?*. Mixing cruelty and comedy, Polanski had conceived of Nancy as a combination of Sade's Justine and *Playboy*'s Little Annie Fanny. In *Macbeth*, Polanski removed Lady Macbeth's clothing to make her more vulnerable. In *What?*, Nancy loses articles of clothing as she moves from scene to scene, intensifying her humiliation. She is there to submit unquestioningly to successive acts of desire.

The problem with *What?* is that it all seems trivial and banal. Bedecking the villa with works of modernist art—as Polanski does—fails to provide the film with the cultural credentials he clearly sought. If *What?* fails as an aesthetic object, it is still fascinating as a cruelly debasing self-parody, in which the Polanskian vision of sadomasochism and violence is deflated. This time, Romek's joke is at his own expense. *What?* is shot through with autobiographical implications, an embarrassing subtext in which the director takes an ironic look at himself and his image. Those who called the film an "in joke" weren't wrong. Polanski provides a key by playing a role: Mosquito, an epithet bestowed on him at the film festival in Rio de Janeiro in 1969 because of his size and irritating behavior.

Mosquito's entrance in *What?* is an obnoxious explosion. Nancy is talking about Alex: "Perhaps he had a difficult childhood." "What about me?" Mosquito shouts. "One shouldn't judge people hastily," she continues. "Sometimes, often, obscure motivations and deep, hidden traumas—" "Trauma, balls!" he snaps.

First, Mosquito seems to ask that his "difficult childhood" be considered, even though "that's no excuse for being a pain in the ass." But the voice of psychology is placed in the mouth of the innocent, making it ridiculous. Having elicited precisely this response, Mosquito gets angry—but in sexual terms, whose conjunction of "trauma" and "balls" hints at the nature of his problem. "They call me Mosquito because I sting with my big stinger." "Pleased to meet you." "What do you think my big stinger is?" "It could mean a lot of things."

If there is innuendo here, it has been planted by Mosquito. But now he mocks the speculation he has elicited, again displaying contradictory impulses. "Yeah, a lot of things, huh?" he says. "You probably think it's something sexual." "Yes," she replies. "Yes," he repeats.

She changes her mind, suspecting he's looking for the contrary response. "No," she says. "No," he repeats. "Not exactly," she concludes, unsure of what he wants her to say. Even *he* seems not to know. This, actually, is a typically Polanskian tactic—to engender innuendo about himself, then to snap at those who pursue its implication.

Like Romek, Mosquito specializes in provocation. It is said that he is a "little brat," a "filthy little freak," and that he's "overexcited for his age, not natural." Later, while the guests at the villa dine, Mosquito arrives, dressed in a bathing suit. "Bunch of creeps!" he shouts, "Never seen me before?"—as he makes an obscene gesture over his groin, so that his finger mimes his penis.

At the meal, he sits beside his enemy, the foppishly dressed Alex, of whose "difficult childhood" Nancy had been speaking. Alex and Mosquito are linked, products of difficult childhoods. But Mosquito detests Alex, mocks his table manners and urbane air. Mosquito is as crude as Alex is genteel.

But Alex is the other of Polanski's self-portraits in *What?* He too dabbles in provocations. The villa teems with visitors, all odd, some threatening; among them, two "lunatics" whom Alex provokes by crushing Ping-Pong balls beneath his foot. The provocation is deliberate, even though Alex knows that toying with the lunatics may mean trouble. There is a painful autobiographical echo in this. The villa, with its open-door policy, suggests the ambience in which Sharon Tate had been killed—and Polanski was still living.

Even more than *Macbeth*, *What?* is most compelling for the personal drama it registers. Throughout Polanski's film-making career, the Polanski image had been taking shape in the mind of his audience. The special world of Polanski, from *Knife in the Water* to *Rosemary's Baby*, was a fully blown version of the thematic obsessions indicated in Romek's student films. After the Manson murders, however, the Polanski image took a new turn: Polanski became known to the general public not just as a filmmaker but as someone associated with *real* violence, even if he had been its victim. His bitter attacks on the press and his bizarre attempt to direct media coverage (the spread in *Life*) suggest the anxiety of the performer suddenly losing control of his public performance. As he had been since his days in the Cracow market square, Romek was the object of attention—but media visibility was not something he could fully manipulate or control. His image was no longer entirely his own creation. *Macbeth* and—more interestingly—*What?* were Polanski's artistic responses to this. Lacking the sure visual taste and style of most of his other films, *Macbeth* and *What?* use the director's public image as raw material —something he would do with far greater control and subtlety in *The Tenant* and *Tess*.

Released in America by Avco-Embassy, *What?* was withdrawn soon after its disastrous premiere. "The decline of any talent is painful to watch," wrote Rex Reed, "but the downfall of Roman Polanski is doubly excruciating because it has been accomplished with so much glee, so much pomposity, and so much public nose-thumbing that it seems almost like a calculated exercise in self-destruction."

Pomposity and nose-thumbing. It was as if Reed were writing about Mosquito. Judith Crist called *What?* "inflated movie making derived from minuscule ideas"—although Braunsberg would claim it had just been "too difficult for American audiences." In *Films and Filming*,

Derek Elley wrote: "At times Polanski seems a little too keen to prod every convention in sight to present his up-side-down world, and much of the dialogue during the first half-hour is needlessly littered with obscenities—like a schoolboy's attempt to shock his elders." Eventually, *What?* would turn up on the porn circuit—recut and reti-tled *Roman Polanski's Forbidden Dreams*—on a double bill with *Eager Beavers*.

thirteen

WHEN ROBERT EVANS screened *What?*, he thought it the worst film he had ever seen. Evans had summoned Polanski to Hollywood with a business proposition, but when Evans disapproved of *What?*, Polanski exploded. *What?* was Polanski straight up, and rejecting it meant rejecting him. Nonetheless, Polanski knew that, after *Macbeth* and *What?*, he needed a commercial success Hollywood-style and Evans could help him get it. So though he carried on when Evans didn't like *What?*, he listened to the proposition anyway.

Evans had signed a contract with Paramount which permitted him to produce his own pictures while remaining vice president in charge of production, and he wanted Polanski to be the first director he backed under the new arrangement. They had talked about the possibility before and had decided to do another literary adaptation because *Rosemary's Baby* had been so successful. Evans sent several properties to Polanski in Europe, but none appealed to him. Now Evans had something else in mind—an original script, *Chinatown*, by Robert Towne, scenarist for *The Last Detail*. Polanski wouldn't have to adapt it—just direct— and Evans thought it a natural for him: so perfect that he had summoned Polanski to look at a rough draft and meet with Towne.

Sixteen months before, when Evans was lunching with Towne, the producer said he was looking for something to produce with his wife, Ali McGraw, starring. Towne replied that he and Jack Nicholson were kicking around ideas for a detective film to be called *Chinatown*. Towne had picked up his title from a buddy who had once been a Los Angeles vice cop. "The one place I never worked was Chinatown," the friend had remarked. "They really run their own culture."

140

Stimulated by this offhand statement, Towne had dreamed up a female character who would embody the enigma of Chinatown even though she was Caucasian. Evans realized that the role was perfect for his wife. Towne built in a role for Nicholson, based on a news article he had read about a divorce detective who stumbled into a maze of political corruption while tagging a woman on assignment. This was all he had so far—a title and two vague characters. Despite the sketchiness of the concept, Evans loved the title and the mood it evoked—and paid Towne to develop it into a script.

Evans wasn't just gambling on an unknown: Towne had written *The Last Detail* and other film and television scenarios. Eager to be involved with the way his scripts were realized, Towne even thought of directing *Chinatown* himself. But Evans already had Roman Polanski in mind. With his stipend, Towne slowly fleshed out a story to go with the title and characters. Finding some old photos of Los Angeles in the thirties, he decided to make it a period piece and scoured the complete works of Raymond Chandler and reference books on the time. When, after eighteen months, he had something to show, one major factor had changed: Ali McGraw had run off with Steve McQueen. Still, Evans liked what he read and called in Polanski to have a look. Some other actress could be cast as the enigmatic woman.

Polanski was enthusiastic about *Chinatown*—but with reservations. Having been accused of self-indulgence in *What?*, Polanski scored Towne's script as "enormous" and "undisciplined." Towne, he felt, knew how to write perfect dialogue—but the script lacked visual interest. When he met with Towne, the two had differences of opinion. Richard Sylbert speculated that it was a question of "metabolism." Polanski said that Towne had taken so long to write *Chinatown* because he was "sluggish." When Polanski suggested cuts, he said he found Towne "lazy" and resistant to changing what he had written. When Towne rewrote, the next draft wasn't much different from the original.

Polanski had never directed a script written completely by someone else; he had always adapted or written it himself or in collaboration. "Look, Bob, I'm taking over," he announced to Towne—and worked on the scenario for two months, although he doesn't get a screenwriting credit. Most detective films, he felt, were convoluted, even incomprehensible, so he streamlined Towne's action and excised characters. By limiting the point of view to the detective, Polanski hoped to replicate the subjectivity of the first person narration in Chandler's novels. Discarding Towne's conclusion, he left the finale open, deciding to work on it later.

After the libidinous excesses of *What?*, the iron-clad order required by the detective genre appealed to Polanski. As Evans had intended, not only his own constant presence on *Chinatown* would discipline Polanski, ordering his impulses, but the natural rigors of the detective genre would be equally bracing. The formulaic movement from dissolution to solution—the guarantee of a radiant finale where mysteries are solved and the threat of crime and chaos dispelled—is what makes the genre so appealing. But Polanski couldn't resist cheating just a bit. When shooting commenced, the ending hadn't been written. In this most conventional and repressive of genres, the ending would be left to instinct and momentary desire.

Towne had written *Chinatown* for Jack Nicholson, who had been his roommate, so the role of the detective, J. J. Gittes, was filled from the start. Part of Polanski's interest in *Chinatown* was a chance to work with Nicholson, whom he had said for some time he wanted to direct. Nicholson had been too little known when Polanski shot *Rosemary's Baby* to get the part of Guy. In the meantime, as Nicholson's star had risen, neither *Macbeth* nor *What?* had been right for him.

For *Chinatown*, Nicholson needed the proper look. Designer Anthea Sylbert judged that the Los Angeles detective would be influenced in his attire by popular movie star styles. His clothing, she thought, would reflect "an outsider's idea of how a star would dress." Before designing Nicholson's costumes, Sylbert scrutinized period photos of male stars at leisure.

Because of Polanski's rewriting, the detective is present throughout the film. The required regimen was exhausting for Nicholson, who felt *Chinatown* was crucial for his career and didn't want to blow the chance. To elicit the performance he wanted, Polanski was not above giving line readings to Nicholson, acting out the role for him. Watching this, Anthea Sylbert "kept waiting for Jack to do his lines with a Polish accent." Actors can be sensitive about line readings, fearing the director is controlling the performance too much. "How do you like those line readings?" Nicholson asked actress Diane Ladd, who was playing the supporting role of Ida Sessions.

"Well," she replied, "he didn't give me line readings, Jack."

"He didn't?"

"No, does he give you line readings?"

"Hell yes, he does."

"And you take it?"

"Well," Nicholson said, "the bastard's my friend. What am I gonna do? But I don't like it."

"Well, you didn't hear him give *me* line readings," Ladd teased.

"You're bull-shittin', Ladd."

"I am not."

"I thought he talked to you before."

"He didn't talk to me before. But *you're* taking line readings, Jack—"

"Yes," he said, "because he's a genius. The little bastard's a genius."

"So what are you complaining about?"

Because Polanski rarely evinces enthusiasm for a performance during shooting, Nicholson grew edgy, worn down by the grueling schedule and lack of response. Polanski exploded one afternoon at Nicholson's immersion in a basketball game on TV when he was supposed to be working. Polanski whacked the screen with a metal bar, but it didn't break. Turning red with anger, Nicholson tore off his clothes, right there on the set. Polanski's assistant tried to cool things, but both men were too hysterical to go back to work. Instead, Polanski had a drink and took off in his car. Stopped for a red light, he saw Nicholson beside him, in his dilapidated Volkswagen. Nicholson grimaced, Polanski grimaced back, they slapped hands through the open windows, and drove off in different directions.

Polanski cast Faye Dunaway as the enigmatic woman, Evelyn Mulwray, originally slated for Ali McGraw. Like Polanski, Dunaway sorely needed a commercial hit. Since her breakthrough with *Bonnie and Clyde*, her career had gone nowhere. But director and actress clashed almost immediately, Dunaway proving less malleable than Francesca Annis and Sydne Rome had been. "Sometimes you can swim through a part," she told *The New York Times*, "but Evelyn is the most complex character in the movie. I had to know why she was behaving as she did." On the set, Dunaway balked at Polanski's instructions and asked that he discuss nuances of character and motivation. In response, Polanski shrieked contemptuously that the money she earned to act the part was motivation enough. He recoiled from having to explain why he asked her to do things, choosing instead to follow his instincts unquestioningly—and insisting that she do the same.

Dunaway wouldn't be pushed around. As a professional, she didn't want merely to echo Polanski's line readings. She had heard that the director tried enraging his actresses in order to stimulate their performance—and she found this approach insulting. When Polanski told her he had heard that directors found her "difficult" and "a pain in the ass," she exploded, accusing him of capitalizing on gossip.

During the shooting of one scene, Polanski saw that one of Dunaway's hairs was out of place, and he broke it off with his fingers—to her horror. When she complained, Polanski accused her of having a "hair fetish." Irritated on another occasion by the time she spent on makeup, he hid tubes of it to disconcert her. Between takes he declaimed Rimbaud to her in French. The conflict escalated when Dunaway rejected Polanski's commands during a scene and stormed off, refusing to work any longer. Only Robert Evans' intervention got her back—so distressed was she by Polanski's "rigid," dictatorial style.

Dunaway needed to develop an interpretation of her role independent of Polanski. Frustrated, she talked with Robert Towne about *his* sense of the story and its psychological mechanisms. Reaching somewhat for the hieraticism of Garbo or Dietrich, Dunaway professed concern with the enigma at the heart of Evelyn Mulwray, who desperately conceals having copulated with her father and having borne his child. "A great deal of guilt and trauma is involved in that character," Dunaway said. "Evelyn is a woman with an enormously traumatized, complex, mysterious past. She spends her life trying to rectify it and to protect her child. As a result, she develops neurotic behavior." As much as Dunaway struggled to assert her creativity, she knew that Polanski would have final control in editing. Displeased with her insistence on motivation, Polanski called her—not Evelyn Mulwray—"completely neurotic."

Despite the tensions between director and actress, Evans was delighted with the actress's on-screen performance. "I think the look Faye Dunaway has in *Chinatown*," he told fashion-conscious *W* magazine, "will be the look for next year. It's sexy . . . chic . . . mysterious."

Polanski was working *against* his material—his script and the talent of his actors—in a struggle to subordinate it to his own vision and obsessions. For everything seemed to be working against *him*, checking his more anarchic impulses. Having stripped down the scenario, Polanski emphasized latent visual motifs—especially the Polanskian theme of voyeurism. Dialogue was left intact: this was Towne's specialty, not Polanski's. The director's preoccupations lay elsewhere—in furtive glimpses of sexual scenes.

Polanski's aesthetic failure in *What?* resulted from a lack of tension with his material. Without narrative interest, Polanski lost his viewers, and critics complained that the film didn't move. In *Chinatown*, the detective story *moves*, but Polanski subtly retards the action—and personalizes it—by inserting still photos, frozen tableaux with overt or latent sexual content. As Antonioni understood in *Blow-Up*, still photos in a film subvert the narrative flow from within. Implicitly, still images do violence to a movie by cutting a moment from time. They are disturbing because they suggest the illusory, fantastic nature of the film we are watching.

Chinatown begins with a series of stills—a couple locked in intercourse. A woman lies on the ground, her panties pulled below her knees, her dress bunched above her waist. Astride her, a man—fully dressed in trousers, jacket, hat. They are frozen, lifeless, although he appears to have penetrated her. On the soundtrack—disembodied groans, as if in parodic accompaniment to the static scene. More images follow. The camera has caught the man and woman in the act, though they don't know it. A hand is shuffling the photos, like some primitive film. The groaning goes on and now the camera pulls back so that we see a man looking at the photos as the detective watches him. In the final image the cuckolded client sees his wife on all fours. Her partner penetrates from behind, his hat still secure on his head.

More photos turn up in *Chinatown*. Taking pictures covertly and then scrutinizing them for clues to sexual mysteries, Gittes is yet another Polanskian voyeur. One of the most effective sequences occurs when the detective spies on a man's secret meeting with a young girl. Gittes is perched above the unsuspecting pair, and we look down at them from his point of view. Noticeably varying distance and camera angle is a cinematic device for making a scene more suggestive, to indicate that it is of special significance. But Polanski doesn't stop there. Next we look directly at Gittes, his face concealed behind a camera. In an extraordinary image, the man and the girl are reflected in the lens. Distorted in reflection, their encounter is shown to be strange, unnatural. The shot is a perfect emblem for voyeurism, the use of the camera to glimpse the forbidden.

In a notorious cameo, Polanski himself plays the detective's nemesis, a repulsive character similar to the bully he played in *Two Men and a Wardrobe*. Gittes is snooping about in the dark, trying to find some clues to the case he is working on, when a voice is heard: "Hold it there, kitty cat. Hold it!" It is Polanski. Unmistakably. Gittes looks up. "Hi!" he says, seeing a big man—and a very little one. "Where'd you get the midget?" The midget isn't amused. He produces a switchblade. "You're a very nosy fellow, kitty cat," he snaps. "Want to guess what happens to nosy fellows?" The knife is shoved up Gittes's nostril. The hand jerks. "They lose their noses." Skin rips, blood gurgles. As usual in Polanski, cruelty is coupled with a joke. Gittes spends much of the film dashing about with an awkwardly bandaged nose.

Relieved by the relative lack of violence in *Chinatown*, critics cited Polanski's cameo as the exception. In the credits, Polanski's role is identified only as the "man with the knife," a witty allusion to his first feature film. When before the filming Anthea Sylbert had sketched the figure, Polanski had balked, not at the costume, but at the face: he wanted it to be just like his. The cameo crystallized what was, by then, the Polanski image—an irrevocable association with violence and crime.

Even more than the cameo, *Chinatown*'s mock resolution is Polanski's mark, a perverse twist on the detective genre. Till almost the end, Evelyn guards a secret. She's been raped by her father, Noah Cross (John Huston). Her daughter is also her half sister. Now Cross wants the child, his daughter and granddaughter. The secret is blurted to Gittes, who sends mother and child into hiding in Chinatown.

While shooting, Polanski had been mulling over the conclusion. He had scrapped Townes's ending in which Evelyn was allowed to escape and decided to write something new. "Make me a Chinese street," he told production designer Richard Sylbert, "a street in Chinatown." The action to occur there wasn't written. Polanski envisioned the ending as an "opera's finale" in which the cast reappears on stage. In his last-minute scenario, Evelyn Mulwray is killed by a cop, and Cross skips off with the child—while Gittes looks on, passive, impotent. Conventionally, detective stories end in the restitution of social order as subversive elements are dispelled. But in Polanski's travesty of the genre, violence and desire triumph.

When it opened, Archer Winsten wrote that *Chinatown* demonstrated "the total Americanization of Roman Polanski." Unlike *What?*, *Chinatown* was a slick, seamless Hollywood product—despite the Polanskian touches, the photos, the cameo and the conclusion. Polanski was playing the game again—and winning. "Once again," wrote Rex Reed, "he proves that with the right material and the right producer to ride herd on his excesses and tendencies toward pretentiousness, he is capable of brilliant work as a creative filmmaker." But Polanski didn't consider *China-town* important—just a way of making himself bankable. He wanted to make more-personal films—and needed the money to do it.

fourteen

POLANSKI LIKED working with Nicholson so much that he proposed another project to him, a big-budget costume film called *Pirates*, which he had coscripted with Gerard Brach. This time, Polanski would play a major role, opposite Nicholson. Everything seemed right for financial backing: Nicholson accepted the idea, and *Chinatown* was a hit. Still, producer Andrew Braunsberg had difficulty attracting sufficient funds. *Pirates* was going to be an expensive, high-risk film—and backers were wary because Polanski would be working both sides of the camera. When Nicholson had to drop out because of other commitments, he was replaced by Robert Shaw, who had appeared in *Macbeth*. But Shaw wasn't as bankable as Nicholson, making the package even less appealing to investors. When the money Polanski needed couldn't be raised, Shaw also dropped out, to appear in *The Deep*, based on Peter Benchley's novel.

Temporarily unable to make *Pirates*, despite the dues he had paid with *Chinatown*, Polanski shifted to a low-budget project, an adaptation of Roland Topor's novel *The Tenant*. He would direct *and* act—but the whole production concept would require a much smaller scale than *Pirates*. Topor, whom Polanski had known for years, had suggested the project to him shortly after *Repulsion*. But since the study of festering madness had struck Polanski as too similar to what he had just done, *The Tenant* was put on hold.

Polanski strongly identified with the novel's main character, Trelkovsky, a paranoic alien in hostile Paris, and had wanted to play him even if someone else directed. Now, frustrated over *Pirates*, he found *The Tenant* exactly the kind of personal film he wanted to make. Because he had just become a naturalized French citizen, the subject matter was more relevant than ever. After coming to the West, Polanski had kept his Polish passport, but the inconve-

149

nience of obtaining visas had led him to apply for French citizenship. Still, he was conscious of his status as a stranger in xenophobic France. Like him, Trelkovsky is newly naturalized and sensitive to reminders that he isn't *really* French. "In Paris," Polanski told the New York *Daily News,* "one is always reminded of being a foreigner. If you park your car wrong, it is not the fact that it's on the sidewalk that matters, but the fact that you speak with an accent."

Although Polanski felt that he and Trelkovsky were "physically very close," there were, he thought, important differences. Trelkovsky is passive and sheepish and responds to hostility by cowering. Polanski found this behavior "self-destructive," he told *Le Monde.* While sharing Trelkovsky's problems, he had chosen to respond to them with his own aggressions. This, for Polanski, constituted the key distinction between Trelkovsky and himself—and he carefully emphasized it in the film. For Polanski, *The Tenant* was a calculated audacity, an attack on a nation of which he had just become a citizen—something the timid Trelkovsky would never have done. In the French press, he reminded his new countrymen of how they had treated him when he was unknown. He announced that even now —famous and ostensibly accepted by the French—he felt like a "painted bird."

After the discipline of *Chinatown,* Polanski's impulse was to script and shoot *The Tenant* as rapidly as possible. Within two months, he had written a scenario with Brach, completed preproduction details, and begun shooting in Paris—Melvyn Douglas and Shelley Winters were cast, as well as Isabelle Adjani, who'd been a hit in François Truffaut's *The Story of Adele H.* For the director of photography, Polanski selected Sven Nykvist, long identified with director Ingmar Bergman. On Nykvist's suggestion, *The Tenant* was shot with a new remote-control camera, the Louma IV—first developed for filming in submarines— which allowed Polanski to capture the claustrophobic spaces Trelkovsky inhabits. As in *Repulsion,* architecture and setting were to provoke and reflect diseased states of mind. Having shot *Persona* for Bergman, Nykvist was experienced in filming psychic dissociation and painstakingly manipulated the lighting and the pictorial composition to achieve the proper atmosphere for Trelkovsky's break-down.

For six weeks, shooting took place at various locations—hospitals, cafes and an exterior in the seedy Pigalle district—and in the Epinay Studios, where designer Pierre Guffroy constructed the grisly interior of the five-story building in which Trelkovsky lives. "I know that atmosphere of the Parisian apartment building," Polanski said, "with the twin menaces of the concierge on the ground floor and the landlord upstairs." Guffroy sought the exact details for each crucial part of the building. The concierge (Shelley Winters) was given the usual old sewing machine and bird cage. The quarters of the landlord, Monsieur Zy (Melvyn Douglas), were densely furnished in predictable Henri II style. But the most effective feature of the set was the building's courtyard, across which Trelkovsky could view the communal toilet from his window. Like the stylized setting for Hitchcock's *Rear Window*, the courtyard in *The Tenant* is ideal for spying—as well as a metaphor for theatricality. When Trelkovsky commits suicide by leaping from the window, the courtyard becomes a theater, complete with boxes and stage.

As Gittes had been a demanding role for Nicholson, so Trelkovsky was for Polanski, necessitating his constant presence before the camera. He found it demanding to concentrate on acting while, as director, he had to attend to other performances and visual details at the same time. Following his accustomed approach, Polanski ordered many takes for each sequence in a struggle to achieve precision. Still, the rushed pace of scripting and shooting allowed Polanski to operate on instinct, in ways forbidden in *Chinatown*. Even more than *What?*, *The Tenant* is the most personal of films, in which Polanski explores impulses submerged in a more finished work like *Chinatown*. Jerzy Skolimowski, Polanski's collaborator on *Knife in the Water*, thought that *The Tenant* made everything else worth it—the humiliations, the disappointments, the compromises. At last, Polanski had fully theatricalized himself, had externalized his fears and fantasies on celluloid.

Although flagrantly crude in both subject matter and

treatment, the notorious drag sequences in *The Tenant*—in which Polanski dons female clothing, makeup and a wig—were not new for him. He had, of course, appeared in drag before, in *When Angels Fall,* and transvestism is one of the favored diversions of the couple in *Cul de Sac.* Polanski's interest in drag reflects an inclination to experiment with identity. Trelkovsky's metamorphosis into Simone Choule, the suicidal previous occupant of his apartment, allows Polanski to ask serious questions about the self and its limits.

When Trelkovsky discovers the vacant flat, Simone isn't yet dead and must expire before he can move in. He visits her in the hospital, where she lies, completely encased in gauze—a mummy with one staring eye and a gaping hole of a mouth, from which a front tooth is missing. Simone's lesbian lover, Stella (Isabelle Adjani), hovers over the bed asking, "Don't you recognize me, Simone?" The mummy shrieks in response, its black mouth straining grotesquely. Invisible beneath her wrappings, Simone is identified with the terrifying hole from which her shriek is emitted.

In the following sequences, attention is called to Trelkovsky's manhood and his fears of castration. Trelkovsky and Stella leave the hospital and go for a drink. At the cafe, he repairs to the toilet, where he is shown urinating. Later, at the movies, Stella fondles his crotch, as a weirdo leers at them from the row behind. These two scenes would be inconsequential if not for a third, in which the threat of castration is openly broached—in anticipation of Trelkovsky's sexual metamorphosis. Trelkovsky and Stella are in bed, and she is eager to consummate their relationship. But he is drunk and rambles anxiously as she undresses him: "At what precise moment does a man cease to be what or who he thinks he is? If I cut off my arm, I can say, 'Me and my arm,' but if I cut off my head, do I say, 'Me and my head?' or 'Me and my body'? What right has my head to call itself me?" Absent from Topor's novel, this meditation alludes to castration anxieties as Stella pulls off Trelkovsky's trousers and his thighs are bared.

The threat of castration is realized when Trelkovsky *becomes* Simone. At first people confuse him with Simone, forcing him to take her mail, eat her customary breakfast, smoke her brand of cigarettes. Then he begins to wear her clothes, left behind in the flat. Increasingly deranged, he buys a wig and high-heeled shoes and makes up his face. Awakening in female attire, Trelkovsky discovers blood on his hands and on the bed. Certain that his deepest fears have come true, he searches frantically for the missing part —a front tooth, whose lack makes him Simone's double.

Besides this, Trelkovsky develops a mysterious bond with a beautiful little girl who lives in the building. He first encounters her at Simone's funeral. Seated across the aisle from him, she gazes at Trelkovsky with recognition, although they have never met. One night, shortly after he has moved into the flat, he discovers Simone's letters, a pair of nylons, bright red nail varnish, a cache of makeup and a yellowed bra. As he holds the bra before him, inspecting it with fascination, there is a knock at the door. Harassed earlier by his new neighbors for making too much noise, he dreads further contact with them but answers anyway. An old woman and the long-tressed little girl have come to see him. As the child gazes passively ahead, her mother laments that they are being persecuted by the other tenants. The general hostility toward the little girl links her to Trelkovsky, who is also ostracized by his neighbors, despite his passive nature. A further link is established when another neighbor, Madame Dios, turns up later to solicit Trelkovsky's signature on a petition to evict the old woman and *her son*. Trelkovsky is perplexed: "Are you absolutely certain she doesn't have a young daughter?" he asks. No, Madame Dios assures him, it is a boy. Trelkovsky's sexual ambiguity is reflected in the little girl/boy, hence the initial gaze of recognition. Not yet a woman, a little girl lingers on the hazy borderline between sexes.

Trelkovsky's fullest identification with the child occurs just before his suicide. Dressed in drag, he sits by the window, through which he has regularly spied on the communal toilet opposite. From the courtyard below, a ball bounces up and down, metamorphosing into a replica of Trelkovsky's made-up, bewigged head. Curious, Trelkovsky peers into the courtyard, where mother and child are being tortured by the neighbors—a sadistic scene and again one not in Topor's novel. Tied up, the old woman is pushed and poked—while the child is restrained and forced into costume. As Trelkovsky observes—silently and passively—the mob covers her face with a mask, whose contours are his, without makeup or wig. Atop the mask, they position a red jester's cap. From this moment, the voyeur's invisibility is challenged: wearing *his* face, the child points an accusing finger at him—calling out with his own voice, dubbed in.

Trelkovsky's sexual ambiguity—his preoccupation with the castration threat—has drawn him to the little girl, whose own ambiguity fascinates him. The voyeuristic impulse is often associated with gazing at the genitals, inspecting size and shape. The diminutive Trelkovsky identifies with the child's borderline status—but also with her humiliation, signified by the jester's guise.

In the language of perversion, voyeurism and exhibitionism are paired. The voyeur imaginatively places himself in the scene he watches—and stages. In *The Tenant,* Polanski makes clear this reciprocity when the voyeuristic Trelkovsky prepares to leap from his window: the courtyard becomes a theater; its windows, little boxes crowded with applauding spectators.

When *The Tenant* opened in France, Polanski complained, in typical fashion, that critics were reviewing him, not his movie. Yet he admitted that he and Trelkovsky were "physically very close" and that he identified with him. He told *Le Monde* that *The Tenant* was a "mature" work in which he returned to the concerns and "symbolism" of the early shorts. On examination, images from them reappear here—a window, a toilet, a transvestite Polanski. More importantly, the themes of voyeurism and the reciprocity between victim and victimizer are reworked and developed. That the voyeur projects himself into his object, inevitably female, is made clear in the conclusion, a parodic replay of the earlier scene in the hospital. Having jumped from the window, like Simone, Trelkovsky finds himself encased in gauze in the hospital bed, being visited by Stella—and his double. Outside, looking in, Trelkovsky is male. Trapped inside, looking out, Trelkovsky is female, unmistakably identified by the gaping hole of the mouth, with its missing tooth.

The voyeur's imaginative projection is also suggested in

the montage in the special issue of the French *Vogue* which Polanski guest-edited after making *The Tenant*. In its layout, Polanski mixed wistful childhood photos, stills from his films, and portraits of actresses he had directed. The last film still is from *The Tenant*—Polanski in drag—followed by a catalogue of actresses, from Deneuve to Tate, with the glaring exception of Kwiatkowska. This juxtaposition of himself as transvestite and his screen women hints at the director's identification with them and the scenes they enacted for him. Polanski also included scenes from "his new passion," the yet unmade *Pirates,* in which a teenaged girl is seen in postures of submission—clutched at the neck by a shaggy buccaneer or merely the object of varied lascivious gazes. The beautiful fifteen-year-old victim is Nastassia Kinski, with whom Polanski was romantically involved.

fifteen

IN HIS ISSUE of the French *Vogue*, Polanski included playful photos of himself at Maxim's, the most fashionable of spots, where he smoked cigars, wore a Ted Lapidus tie, and dined on champagne and caviar. The French *Vogue* connoted good taste and fashion: his guest-editorship meant he had become an arbiter, even if he viewed the role with irony. The newly naturalized Frenchman hadn't forgotten his Polish past, as the album of old photos, ranging from childhood to young manhood, made clear. Also, the stills from his Polish films known in the West—*Two Men and A Wardrobe, Mammals* and *Knife in the Water*—were prominently labeled with their original Polish titles.

Polanski was thinking about his youth, the world he had left behind, and announced to a correspondent from the Polish newspaper *Polityka* that he wanted to return there for a while: "I'd like to visit Poland," he said, "where I haven't been for about fifteen years. I've promised this trip to myself for a long time, but professional obligations kept me away. This time, I've definitely decided to go."

In December 1976, Roman Polanski left his adopted land for Poland. He would be coming home in triumph—*the* Polish director who had made it in the West. From Paris he would fly to Warsaw, to change planes for the trip to Cracow. But air travel in the East can be difficult in winter, and Polanski's flight from Paris was diverted to Prague, Czechoslovakia, because of heavy fog. Polanski was too anxious and impatient to linger in a hotel and sent word to his father that he had rented a car and planned to drive all night to Cracow.

When he got to Cracow, it was six in the morning. He drove through the city to the slightly shabby building near the main marketplace where his father and Wanda lived. As he pulled up, he could see parked in front the incongruous navy blue Mercedes-Benz he had given Ryszard. Upstairs in Apartment Number 7, Ryszard showed him a bed, in which he could sleep for a few hours. He did not sleep long. That afternoon, he took the keys to the Mercedes and disappeared, without telling his father where he was going. When a few hours had passed, his father became worried—after all, the son hadn't been home for fifteen years—and called Renek Nowak.

"Renek, is Romek there?" he blurted into the phone. For Ryszard, his son was still Romek, still difficult: nothing had changed. Renek had been Romek's boyhood friend, and his modest apartment was stuffed with Polanski memorabilia —blurry photos, letters, even old report cards. Over the years, old Ryszard had gotten into the habit of talking to Renek as if he were still his son's intimate friend—an assumption Nowak didn't discourage, since he half-believed it himself. Now Ryszard was certain that Renek would know where Romek had gone. "You must know where he is!" But Renek didn't. "He took my Mercedes," Ryszard continued, "and he's been gone for seven hours!" Finally, the Mercedes pulled up in front, and Romek was back, having visited a tiny peasant village outside Cracow where he had lived as Roman Wilk during the war.

Renek, ebullient at Romek's return to Poland and eager to bask in reflected glory, ushered his old friend as quickly as possible to the market square, Cracow's most public place, where Romek used to perform. When one of the old habitués of the square nodded quietly while passing by, Renek stopped him. "Don't you know who *this* is?" he barked.

"Of course," replied the man, "it's Romek Polanski."

"But aren't you surprised to see the famous director Roman Polanski back in Cracow after all these years?"

The man seemed puzzled. What was Renek talking about? Yes, the man had read about the famous director in the papers—but had always assumed that it was some other "Polanski," not the practical joker he had known.

Romek stayed with his father and stepmother in Cracow for Christmas, then went to Warsaw to meet with the film-makers who had remained behind. Although he was feted by the Warsaw film community, there was some antipathy toward him among those who thought he had betrayed Poland in his move to the West, particularly because he had become a French citizen.

In Warsaw, Romek stayed with leading director Janusz Morgenstern and his wife, Krystyna, both old friends. Jerzy Skolimowski escorted Romek about, but there was tension between the one time collaborators. When Polanski left Poland, Skolimowski had originally stayed behind, making cerebral, innovative films that brought him an international reputation. The odds were that he would be even more successful than Polanski. But when Skolimowski went West—teaming up on *Adventures of Gerard* with Polanski's former partner and producer Gene Gutowski—his career faltered, his attempts at commercial filmmaking temporarily dampening the sensibility that had made his earlier work so successful. (Only later, in 1978, would Skolimowski make a first-rate film in the West: *The Shout*, with Alan Bates—proving that he was still a force to reckon with.) When Polanski visited in 1976, Skolimowski hadn't made a film in several years and was living with his wife and two sons in a one-room flat, having run out of funds to finish his villa, which lay half-completed. Polanski's arrival reminded Skolimowski of his own disappointments and his continuing ambitions for building a successful career in the West.

As New Year's Eve approached, it seemed that everyone was inviting Romek to a different party. All his old friends wanted to be regaled with stories of success, glamour, Hollywood and the movie stars. They wanted to know about Jack Nicholson and Catherine Deneuve and Mia Farrow and Warren Beatty. Even those cynics who whispered that Romek had sold out were curious about him. The Morgensterns' phone rang so often that it finally had to be disconnected.

As Romek party-hopped, the most beautiful women in Warsaw struggled to catch his attention, to make him stop and look. But Romek had eyes for only one of them—the sixteen-year-old daughter of a friend. Everyone noticed it, but no one was surprised. Romek's taste for the young was common knowledge. Still, one drunken woman, throwing her arms around his neck, refused to let go. Amused at the theatrical possibilities of the situation, Romek paraded across the dance floor with the limp admirer clinging to him. He greeted old friends and swapped memories, talking over and around the body whose feet had come to rest on his. Romek didn't want to talk about Hollywood or the other things everyone was asking about. Nearly smothered beneath his inert companion, he reminisced about Poland, reeling off the most trivial details of the past: names of girlfriends and waitresses, clothes, motorcycles—every image he could recall.

But the film community had hard questions to ask. Besides hearing the latest gossip from Hollywood, people wanted to know *why* Romek Polanski had been a hit in the West. Why had no other Polish director succeeded as he had? They had a chance to grill him when he spoke before the Warsaw film club on January 3. Five hundred people jammed into the meeting hall. Journalists scribbled notes; photographers snapped pictures. Prominent filmmakers, critics and other artists and intellectuals milled in the crowd, waiting for Romek. Finally he appeared, accompanied by the club's president, Andrzej Slowicki, who introduced him as *"the* most famous of Polish directors"—a description sure to arouse the audience.

Instead of making a speech, Romek proposed that the audience ask questions, which, he told them, he was certain would be "very mean" and "very personal"—"But I'm not afraid of *anything*," he assured them. For a moment, silence swept the room. This was the old, provocative Romek talking, creating a situation, egging on the audience. No one knew how to respond. Was he joking? Did he mean to be ironic? Or was he mocking them? There was no telling.

Finally someone called out a question: "Why did you come?"

"Because I wasn't here for a long time," he answered.

Now the questions and comments took off—touching on a wide range of topics. "Well, I can see how worldly you are," Romek told them, "and I was prepared to take you for a bunch of provincials."

Naturally, the question of Romek's "Polishness"—or lack of it—was brought up, a sensitive subject on both sides. "I think your films are not very Polish," Romek was told. "You're the only Polish director who has proved himself in America precisely because you're not *really* Polish!"

Romek assured the audience that he had kept dual citizenship in France *and* Poland—but this didn't satisfy them.

"I read in *Newsweek*," someone called out, "that you said you don't know whether you're French."

"What are you getting at?" Romek snapped.

"What you said in *Newsweek*."

"If you're so *worldly*, all of you, you should know what I said in *Newsweek!*"

After his scandalous conduct with Komeda, the last thing Romek wanted to be asked about was the composer's death; so when someone wondered whether the loss of Komeda had had a detrimental effect on Polanski's films, Romek changed the subject, talking generally about movie music, without ever mentioning Komeda.

"Why hasn't Skolimowski worked for so long?" came another question. "Ask him," replied Romek.

By now, everyone had noticed that Skolimowski had not yet turned up. His seat was vacant, and people wondered why, whispering among themselves. Charges of commercialism nettled Romek, who claimed that success and seriousness weren't mutually exclusive. "I'd rather see a good commercial film where I'm not bored for two hours," he insisted, "than some pseudo-intellectual French film."

"Why did you make *Macbeth*?" someone shouted. "To measure yourself against Shakespeare?"

"Aren't you afraid," asked another, "that you haven't made a statement in your films—and that now it might be too late?"

"I know what you're getting at," Romek retorted. "I know, sir, that you're making fun of me. But I'm interested in life as much as you—and maybe more, because I have more occasion to experience life." Accused of shallowness, of making films without intellectual substance, Romek flouted the privileges of his success.

"Is it easy to make money in the West?" a woman cried out.

"No," replied Romek, "it's very difficult."

Pressed on the issue of having sold out, Romek was adamant: "I can only say that whatever my life and work have been, I'm not envious of *anyone*—and this is my biggest satisfaction."

There was a commotion at the back of the hall, then a burst of applause as Jerzy Skolimowski strode down the aisle to take his seat. He was as lithe and handsome as ever —wearing a frilly silk scarf that only an ex-boxer with a broken nose could get away with.

"I have a question," a voice shouted from the audience, Skolimowski having stolen their attention. "Why doesn't Mr. Polanski have a silk scarf?"

Romek fumbled for words. The jibe was ambiguous—but it stung. Skolimowski was the home team, and the audience was with him, not Polanski, the visitor. Now someone mentioned Andrzej Wajda, the most esteemed of Polish directors. "Wajda titled one of his films *Everything for Sale*," the voice began. "I would like to ask if you think everything is for sale. Do you have any limits? Are there any tragedies in your life you wouldn't use to sell a film?"

Romek's encounter with the Polish cinéastes had prompted another of his provocative performances. Like Mosquito in *What?*, he played the crowd to stir up their feelings. Although some of the questioners implied that Romek had sold out in the West, he had never really fitted into the serious socially and politically engaged Polish cinema. From the first, his amoral vision had provoked people's confusion and anger. Now his friends sat quietly as he and the audience went at each other. This was the way it had always been with Romek.

The session at the film club was trying for Romek, but another grilling was yet to occur. Before leaving Warsaw, he gave an interview to Janusz Glowacki for the influential weekly *Kultura*. The title Glowacki fashioned for the published interview—"Polo Potrafi"—was a pun on a political slogan then recently coined by Edward Gierek, then head of the Polish Communist party—"Polak Potrafi" (Poles can do it). Gierek's slogan referred to the determination of the Polish people to overcome economic hardship. Glowacki's title substituted "Polo" (a Polanski nickname), ironically suggesting Romek's determined struggle for success.

"Why did you leave Poland?" Glowacki asked.

"Why did Erich von Stroheim leave Germany?" Romek shot back. "Why did Hitchcock leave England? If you were a director you'd like to work in Hollywood too. Now go ahead and ask me if I'm still Polish. You people keep asking me this question. You want Polish artists to make it in the world, but when they do, you accuse them of treason." Pressed about whether he felt himself successful, Romek said, "I never made a film which fully satisfied me."

"Why?"

"If I knew, I'd make it."

"Do you think you'll find out making *Pirates*?"

"You treat commercial films as treason," Romek said, "but millions of people want to see them."

"But what do *you* want?"

"I want people to go to the movies. I am the man of the spectacle. I'm playing."

"But aren't you playing with yourself?" Now Glowacki abruptly changed the subject. "Did you ever love anybody?" he asked.

"A few women."

"But normal love doesn't figure in your films."

"Because normal love isn't interesting," Romek explained. "I assure you that it's incredibly boring. And, as I said, I love spectacles."

sixteen

WHEN POLANSKI returned to Paris, he accepted an assignment from *Vogue Hommes,* a sophisticated French men's magazine, to shoot a glossy photo spread on little girls of the world. Still unable to secure financing for *Pirates,* Polanski signed a development deal with Columbia Pictures to script and direct an adaptation of Lawrence Sanders' *The First Deadly Sin,* a best-seller about a psychotic killer. He decided to work on the scenario and gather candidates for the kiddie spread in California. While in Paris, his friend Henri Sera reminded him of a woman Sera had introduced him to the year before in a Los Angeles bar. A minor actress, she had two daughters. Sera was dating one of them and suggested her younger sister, then thirteen, as a potential model.

Arriving in Los Angeles, Polanski checked into the Beverly Wilshire Hotel and telephoned the woman's home in Woodland Hills in the San Fernando Valley no less than eleven times. On February 13, Polanski drove his rented Mercedes to visit mother and child and make his pitch. Ushering him into the living room, the attractive woman, in her thirties, told Polanski that the child was waiting in her bedroom, so they could talk. As credentials, Polanski brought the issue of French *Vogue* he had guest-edited. The photos of Nastassia Kinski had an erotic undertone, but she *was* fully clothed—and the mother had the impression that Polanski would be photographing her child for French *Vogue,* an exciting prospect because of the magazine's status and influence. But French *Vogue* is a fashion magazine *for women,* different in tone and audience from its often erotic counterpart, *Vogue Hommes.*

When Polanski mentioned that he was looking for an eleven-year-old, the mother admitted that her daughter was thirteen, perhaps too old for his needs. Polanski said he would have a look anyway, and the candidate was summoned before him. Sera had been right: she was perfect. Polanski set a date, February 20, for a photographing session. Recollecting this initial meeting, the mother would hit upon an important fact: they had discussed the child's age. Polanski *knew* she was thirteen.

A week later, Polanski was back, armed with cameras and equipment. The first session took place behind the house, but when the mother asked to watch, Polanski suggested that this would "inhibit" her daughter, so she left them alone. After a few routine shots, Polanski asked the child to remove her blouse but assured her that he would crop the photos to avoid showing her "boobies," as he called her breasts. Polanski didn't think topless photography improper, since it is common in Europe. But the child was dubious enough not to tell her mother. As far as the woman knew, her daughter had been clothed throughout.

Polanski wasn't excited about *The First Deadly Sin*, because he had made suspense pictures before and now wanted to explore other directions. But after the commercial failure of *The Tenant*—too abstruse for a mass audience—Polanski needed a hit, such as *Chinatown* had been after *What?*, so he forged ahead on the Sanders story. He had hoped to cast Robert De Niro as the psycho in *The First Deadly Sin* because De Niro had impressively played a somewhat similar role in Martin Scorsese's *Taxi Driver*. And according to Shelley Winters, De Niro was also interested in working with Polanski—but on *another* project, *The Deerhunter*, then in production. The controversial Vietnam epic had been director Michael Cimino's brainchild, but with a single prior directing credit, he was constantly threatened with losing control—and De Niro, who was starring in the film, had Polanski in mind to replace him.

Another photography session with the thirteen-year-old was scheduled for March 10, but this time Polanski wanted to take her to the home of a friend on Mulholland Drive. Polanski turned up at Woodland Hills to pick her up and to give the mother his friend's telephone number. A friend of the child was visiting, and the mother assumed that Polanski would take the two of them, but as they got ready to leave, she saw that the friend wasn't getting into the car. She rushed over to ask what had happened. Polanski, the friend said, had told her she couldn't come. The mother watched as Polanski and her daughter drove off together.

Later, when she dialed his friend's number, a woman on the other end of the phone assured her that everything was all right. Other people were present, and Polanski was busy shooting pictures. As the light began to dim, Polanski decided to move to Jack Nicholson's house, also on Mulholland Drive. Nicholson, he knew, was in Aspen, Colorado, and the house was being occupied by his girlfriend, Anjelica Huston. Polanski phoned the Nicholson house, then the child's mother, giving her the new number and assuring her that Anjelica Huston would be present.

When Polanski and his model arrived at Nicholson's, only the caretaker, Helena Kallianiotes, was there. Polanski asked for a drink, and she sent him to the refrigerator, where he found a magnum of champagne.

Later the young model would reconstruct the events that followed. She was confused about sequence and time because she and Polanski had been left alone by Miss Kallianiotes and the champagne went to the thirteen-year-old's head. "I don't know how much, because I was drinking some of his too. I just kept—I just kept drinking it for pictures and, you know." Polanski had begun to shoot more photos. Then he stopped and went into a bathroom. Following him, the girl saw he had a container of pills, one of which was broken into three parts in his hand. "Is this a Quaalude?" he asked. She said yes, telling him that she had once taken a Quaalude, which she had found; it belonged to her older sister. "Do you think I will be able to drive if I take it?" he asked. "Well, I guess I will." Then he swallowed and asked her, "Do you want part?" "No . . . oh, OK," she replied. The champagne and the pill disoriented her.

Polanski photographed her in Nicholson's elaborate Jacuzzi, sometimes topless, sometimes totally nude. In a few shots she clutched glasses of champagne. Then Polanski began to take off his clothes to join her in the Jacuzzi. She was still alert enough to panic and told him they had to call her mother.

The telephone rang at the child's Woodland Hills home, and the mother answered. "Are you all right?" she asked her daughter.

"Uh huh."

"You want me to come and pick you up?"

"No."

After hanging up, the child had second thoughts and decided to fake an asthma attack—a condition from which she did not suffer—and asked Polanski to take her home, saying she was unable to breathe. Instead, he told her to go into a bedroom and lie down. She obeyed, but would later say, "I can barely remember anything that happened . . . I was kind of dizzy, you know, like things were kind of blurry sometimes." Polanski had come into the room and began kissing her. After performing cunnilingus, Polanski penetrated her vaginally, asking her, she recalled, if she used birth control pills and when she had last menstruated. She didn't know how long his penis had been in her vagina, "but not a very long time." He withdrew before ejaculating. Then Polanski penetrated her anally, climaxing in her rectum. At this point, Anjelica Huston returned and knocked at the bedroom door. Polanski got up and went to talk to her. When he returned to the bed, he tried once more to have intercourse with the child. Finally, the two of them got up and dressed, going out to speak briefly with Anjelica Huston before Polanski drove the girl home.

Back in Woodland Hills, she rushed into her house, ahead of Polanski, and as she brushed past her mother, she whispered, "If he asks, tell him I have asthma," then closed herself in her bedroom. The woman's boyfriend—an employee of the periodical *Marijuana Monthly*—and her elder daughter were in the living room, and she invited Polanski to join them. If the girl had acted strangely, Polanski was calm and controlled, offering them a look at the photos from the session in the backyard. Crude and poorly executed, the images weren't what the mother had expected. But when she spotted the topless shots, she grew really disturbed, although she knew Polanski couldn't publish them without a release. No one had the nerve to say anything about the poor quality of the images, and a meek attempt to get Polanski to turn over the topless shots was rebuffed. The encounter grew uncomfortable on both sides, and Polanski packed up his photos and left, after which it occurred to the mother that he had never produced a release form.

In her bedroom the girl called her seventeen-year-old boyfriend and told him what had gone on at Jack Nicholson's house. The boy wasn't sure whether to believe her, but her elder sister did, having listened to every word from the hallway. Shocked, she rushed to tell their mother, who, when she finished listening, called her accountant, asking him to recommend a lawyer. But the lawyer he suggested wasn't at home, and next she dialed the police. Her daughter, she told them, had been raped.

She had called the police without consulting her daughter. The officers who responded escorted the child to Parkland Hospital for an examination. The thirteen-year-old, it seemed, had had two prior sexual experiences, one only two weeks before. She said that Polanski had performed oral sex on her, then penetrated her vaginally and anally, climaxing in her rectum. No blood was found on her garments or perineum, and an anal examination turned up "no evidence of forced entry." There was, however, indication of semen on her panties. The tests were routinely undertaken to determine two things—whether there had been sexual contact and whether force had been used. But in the case of a thirteen-year-old in California, force was not technically an issue, since a child under the law of that state *cannot* consent.

The medical examination completed, the girl and her mother were questioned further by police. "What about the sodomy?" the teenager was asked.

The child looked puzzled. "What do you mean?"

When they had defined it, she seemed to understand.

"Oh," she said, "I just thought he was going in the wrong way."

Since the accused rapist was a public figure, the district attorney's office was called upon to monitor events. James Grodin, a young deputy district attorney, asked to question the victim alone while the mother waited outside with her boyfriend. Grodin found the girl's manner and appearance childish. As she related her story she burst into tears several times. She told him she had attempted to scream in the bedroom at Nicholson's house, but that she was so woozy from champagne and Quaaludes that no sound came out. Grodin came away from the interview convinced that she was telling the truth. But before he ordered an arrest he wanted to be sure that the mother knew what she was getting into and wouldn't back out. He carefully explained to mother and child that a case involving a world-famous director in Hollywood would unleash a flood of publicity. The mother assured him that she knew what they were getting into, that she just wanted Polanski arrested. While the warrant was being sworn out, the mother and her boyfriend conferred with the little girl and agreed to take her to McDonald's for dinner.

The next night, as Polanski prepared to leave the Beverly Wilshire Hotel for the theater, two sets of policemen and two deputy district attorneys were waiting for him in the lobby. The number of police didn't mean anyone expected Polanski to resist arrest. Extra men were needed for the planned search of Jack Nicholson's house for evidence. The deputy district attorneys Grodin and David Wells were there to supervise the arrest. Because Polanski was a VIP, they wanted to make certain everything was done by the book.

When Polanski emerged, accompanied by several friends, men and women, one of the policemen addressed him: "I'd like to speak with you, Mr. Polanski," he said, identifying himself as a police officer. "Is it going to take long?" Polanski coolly asked. Either he suspected nothing, or he was a terrific actor. When the police said it would take a while, the friends around Polanski grew alarmed. "Go on to the theater," he told them, "and either I'll join you there or I won't." He was unruffled, in total control. When the friends protested, he calmly dismissed them, "Go ahead, go to the theater." As they walked off, chattering among themselves and glancing back, Polanski turned to the policeman. "Where do you want to talk?" he asked.

The policeman responded that they had a warrant to search Polanski's room and suggested that they go there. Eyeing the cops and deputy district attorneys, Polanski asked if it was necessary for everyone to go up as a group. These were obviously cops, and Polanski wanted to avoid unnecessary gossip. The police agreed to split into two groups. As they walked toward the elevators, one of the police saw Polanski lift his hand to put something in his mouth. He grabbed Polanski's wrist and took a Quaalude from his palm, the same drug the child claimed he had given her.

In his room Polanski acted like a host, inviting them to sit down. His face was expressionless, his manner polite. He had not yet asked for any explanation. Only now, with the door closed behind them and Polanski seated in an overstuffed easy chair, did he broach the subject. "What's this all about?" he asked. "You know what we're here for," one of the men replied.

Meanwhile, Grodin had spotted a selection of photos and slides scattered upon the dresser as if someone had been casually viewing them. On inspection he saw that they all treated a single subject—young girls. "That's what we're here for," Grodin said, indicating the cluttered dresser top. "We had a report from a young girl that you photographed. She reported that you raped her yesterday." Polanski began to cross and uncross his legs.

Grodin lifted a slide to the light. Polanski jumped up to help, again acting as if these were casual visitors. He offered Grodin a slide viewer, telling him how to operate it. But he was called back to his seat by one of the policemen, who was impatient to question him.

Asked for his side of the story, Polanski inquired, "Are you going to arrest me whether I say anything or not?" But without waiting for the officer's response, Polanski smiled —for the first time—and said, "OK, here it is," and denied everything. The drugs, the rape, the sodomy. Nothing untoward had happened, he claimed.

The police told him that they had to take him downtown for booking. As the photos, slides and undeveloped film were confiscated—to be added to the Quaalude he had tried to swallow and other pills found in his bathroom— Polanski asked if it was necessary for everybody to go down in the elevator together. Wells said he would escort Polan-

ski downtown himself. Grodin and the police searched Polanski's rented Mercedes, then joined them at the station
house.

Afterward, Grodin told Polanski they wanted him to accompany them for the search of Nicholson's house. They
proceeded to Mulholland Drive, where an electric gate
barred access to the compound, which comprised three
houses owned by Marlon Brando, the middle one rented
by Nicholson. There was no response to the buzzer, although Polanski insisted that the maid must be there.
"That's OK," he added, "I know how to get to the other
side." At that, he leaped up and over the gate. "Oh my God,
where's he going?" muttered one of the police while another followed Polanski over the gate. By then Polanski
was on the other side, pushing a button to release the lock.

After much banging on Nicholson's door, Anjelica Huston finally responded, visibly annoyed at the commotion
and unfriendly toward Polanski. It seemed that she had
quarreled with Nicholson and was packing her bags to
leave when the cops turned up to search the premises. Interviewed privately in the kitchen, she said that Polanski
was a "freak." It seemed obvious that she was trying to
make sure that no one associated Nicholson or her with
Polanski. Recounting her return to the house the night before, she said that she had walked about calling, "Roman,
Roman, where are you?" until he responded from the bedroom near the pool. "We're down here!" he shouted. When
she opened the door, she found them "going at it." Polanski
got up and walked over to her, naked from the waist down.
"We'll be out in a few minutes," he said.

About twenty minutes later, the girl emerged, hastily
dressed and clearly a little woozy. "Are you OK?" Huston
asked her. "Yeah, I'm OK, but I want to go right home."

Huston and Polanski talked, then she turned back to the
girl and asked again, "Are you OK?" She replied by asking
to go home. "Roman," asked Huston, "are you going to take
her home?" He said that he would and left with the child
and his equipment. Telling the story in the kitchen, Huston
seemed "really pissed that this had happened"—according
to the law enforcement officer who interviewed her.

Meanwhile, a cop had discovered a large container of

hashish in a drawer in Nicholson's bedroom. Then, in Huston's purse, he found cocaine and announced he would have to "dust for fingerprints." But Huston stopped him. "I'll save you the trouble, because it's my stuff." Now Anjelica Huston too would have to be taken downtown for booking. Eventually she was released on her own recognizance.

But Polanski was detained and became increasingly nervous. "Is this going to take long?" he repeated over and over. "Look," Grodin finally said, "you've got to realize that this is a very serious thing. It's going to take a long time." Then Grodin tried to calm Polanski by changing the subject to movies, announcing that he'd seen *Knife in the Water* twice. Polanski smiled. "You've seen *Knife in the Water* twice? Then you're not a policeman. What are you?" Grodin explained.

After they had talked film, Polanski asked Grodin for one of the confiscated Quaaludes. He explained that the Quaaludes had been prescribed for him for hyperactivity and that he took them regularly to calm down. Grodin refused the request. A temporary lawyer was secured to handle the booking and Polanski's bail. Finally, Polanski was booked on suspicion of unlawful sexual intercourse with a thirteen-year-old girl and was released on $2,500 bail.

The next morning the case hit the papers. Visiting Los Angeles, Polish critic Krzysztof Toeplitz read about Polanski's plight. Two months before, Polanski had lorded it over his Polish friends who had envied his success abroad. Now, Polanski was publicly humiliated, a fallen man. Toeplitz was in town as part of a delegation sent with Poland's official entry for the Oscar for best foreign film, Jerzy Antczak's lengthy historical epic *Nights and Days*. Polanski had been invited to a screening of the film that day, but after reading the news Toeplitz didn't expect him to turn up. Yet when he reached the screening room, there was Polanski— pale and subdued, not his usual active self. The only time Toeplitz had seen Polanski like this was years before, after a car accident on the way to Lodz. When he had gotten out of the car, he stood absolutely still, saying nothing. People joked that he *must* have been in shock to be so quiet.

Jerzy Skolimowski was changing planes at the Frankfurt

Airport, on his way from Warsaw to America. After Polanski's visit to Warsaw, Skolimowski, feeling it was his only remaining gamble, had telephoned Jack Nicholson to ask for help in landing another directing project in the West, and Nicholson had invited him to Aspen. Skolimowski was staking everything on this visit. Rushing through the airport, he glimpsed a fragment of a headline, "Polanski . . . Rape . . . Arrest." Grabbing a newspaper, he dashed to catch his plane. On board he opened it and his heart sank. Besides Romek's fall, he was thinking about himself. The last thing Nicholson would want, he suspected, would be a visit from *another* Pole. But when he got to New York and nervously called Nicholson, he found his invitation was still good and flew on to Colorado. After meeting with the actor, he went to Los Angeles to visit Polanski. He had never seen him like this before, not even when Romek had been dumped by Basia Kwiatkowska for another man.

Polanski's personal crisis infected his professional life when a decision was made at Columbia "not to go forward" with him as director of *The First Deadly Sin*. Polanski had been depending on the deal, and its cancellation caused him serious financial problems. He was paying top dollar for his highly regarded lawyer, Douglas Dalton, but knew that he could not afford to economize on his defense.

The prosecution of the Polanski case was assigned to a young Mormon, Roger Gunson, known as one of the straightest men in the District Attorney's office. When a twenty-one-member Los Angeles County grand jury convened to hear secret testimony, included among the witnesses were the mother, the alleged victim and the seventeen-year-old boy whom she had phoned and first told about the rape. Gunson was worried about the boy and the impression he would make on the Grand Jury. Although the girl's morals were not legally at issue in the case, any sentiment against her could undermine her credibility. Potentially, the admission of prior sexual experience could destroy the case even though, technically, such prior experience had no bearing on the present case. Gunson hadn't interviewed the boy before his Grand Jury testimony and didn't know what he looked like. Unable to pick out a likely looking seventeen-year-old in the courtroom the morning of the hearing, Gunson inquired and was told "It's the young-looking one." The prosecutor was then introduced to the witness, a quiet boy who looked no more than twelve. Gunson was relieved, for the boy's childish appearance would vitiate the threat that the victim's "prior sexual experience" with him could pose for the prosecution's case.

At the hearing Gunson surprised some observers by quizzing the girl about her prior sexual activities. He later disclosed two strategic reasons. First, Gunson raised the issue of the girl's sexual activities in order to obviate any subsequent claims by the defense which might lead to another hearing. Second, Gunson felt that the information the girl would reveal would help her case by countering any rumors there might be of extreme promiscuity.

Another source close to the prosecution revealed that Gunson was concerned about the results of the medical examination at Parkland Hospital which had turned up no evidence of vaginal or anal damage. In a case of rape involving a thirteen-year-old, a juror might expect damage, so by revealing that she wasn't a virgin, Gunson would make such expectations irrelevant.

After a day of listening and deliberating, the Grand Jury handed down a six-count indictment, each count a felony:

COUNT I: "furnishing a controlled substance to a minor";
COUNT II: committing "a lewd and lascivious act" on a child, a 13-year-old girl;
COUNT III: "unlawful sexual intercourse";
COUNT IV: "rape by use of drugs," including Quaalude and alcohol;
COUNT V: "perversion," "copulating the mouth of him . . . with the sexual organ" of the child;
COUNT VI: "sodomy"

If convicted on all six counts, Polanski would face up to fifty years in prison.

When Polanski arrived at the Los Angeles Criminal Court for formal arraignment, a frenzied mob of onlookers awaited. Even a veteran court reporter like Theo Wilson of the New York *Daily News* was stunned by the commotion over the Polanski case. Besides the hundred or so reporters and cameramen struggling to get close to Polanski, Wilson noted, "the pushing, yelling crowd . . . included excited high school kids and a large contingent of the foreign press . . . a spectacle reminiscent of other times." There seemed to be as much interest in a celebrity rape case in the "laid-back" seventies as in the forties when Errol Flynn had come to trial.

Assigned to the case was Superior Court Judge Laurence J. Rittenband. The proceedings were moved from the downtown courthouse to the so-called "celebrity court" in Santa Monica.

While the case was pending, Roger Gunson made a lay-man's investigation into the relationship between art and life of the sort Polanski's cinema has appeared to encourage. In the wake of the publicity surrounding the case, a Santa Monica movie theater ran a weekly Polanski festival, and each Wednesday night the hard-working deputy district attorney scrutinized Polanski's films for clues to the director's psyche. To Gunson as he watched the films, a theme seemed to emerge—that of the conflict between good and evil. Should Polanski admit his guilt while claiming that this had been a one-time aberration, the prosecution could counter by using the films as evidence of the defendant's *consistent* tendencies.

Polanski moved out of the Beverly Wilshire and into the Chateau Marmont Hotel, where he and Sharon Tate had first lived together after their marriage. Shortly after his arrest, he had made a deposit on the purchase of a house in Hollywood Hills, on Rising Glen Road, but the sale fell through. In need of money, Polanski signed a development deal with Italian producer Dino De Laurentiis, who was now operating out of Beverly Hills. Polanski was to script and direct a remake of the John Ford classic *Hurricane*. De Laurentiis had attempted to acquire Polanski's services before, offering him the direction of *King Kong*. But Polanski had turned the project down, telling friends he couldn't work up much interest in a monkey.

Working again, Polanski appeared in court rarely, when motions had to be made in the pre-trial hearings. His French passport hadn't been lifted, because it seemed unlikely that someone who had just accepted a contract to direct a multimillion-dollar movie was going to disappear. With the court's permission, Polanski was able to travel abroad, even making a trip to Bora Bora to scout locations. But Polanski was depressed and insecure. The rape charges had made him a pariah to some people who seemed frightened in his presence and steered away from him.

Polanski insisted to friends that he had dated the mother of the thirteen-year-old, and that the mother had turned him in out of jealousy over his interest in her daughter. He had done nothing wrong, he claimed—at least not by adult European standards. Friends circulated stories about Polanski's having been set up—either by mother or by daughter. One elaborate scenario, offered by Shelley Winters, had the girl setting up Polanski in an attempt to secure a role in *The First Deadly Sin*.

After a series of postponements and motions, both sides put out feelers concerning possible plea-bargaining. But these early attempts failed. The problem remained for Polanski that if he was convicted of a crime of moral turpitude, which the charges involved, he faced the threat of being deported. Because his work as a director necessitated his having access to Hollywood, deportation was something he wished to avoid at all costs.

Dalton had sought to question the girl and to have her psychiatrically evaluated on the chance that she had imagined it all. He also moved to have her panties inspected, claiming that the semen found there might not be Polanski's. These defense motions were denied. Discovering that the press had gotten wind of the failed plea-bargaining attempts, Dalton was concerned because he didn't want the public thinking that Polanski might be willing to admit any guilt in the case. He tried to get Judge Rittenband to issue a gag order forbidding public comment on the case. An alert reporter, Richard Brenneman, learned of the gag-order attempt and wrote a story about it in the local Santa Monica paper, after which, citing the public's right to know, Rittenband denied Dalton's request.

After many postponements, a trial date was set—August 9, the eighth anniversary of Sharon Tate's murder. Gunson and the District Attorney's office had accumulated substantial evidence against Polanski, but the girl's family—which included her mother, her adoptive father and her sister—grew increasingly hesitant about having her testify in open court. In the months since the arrest, they had recoiled at public speculation even while her identity was secret. Although most reporters honored the agreement to suppress her name until the trial, there were exceptions. Within days reporters knew who she was and where she lived, and some turned up at her school to question her classmates, while others staked out her house. One free-lance photographer using a telephoto lens took a picture of the girl and her mother sitting in a car. He sold the photo for five hundred dollars. Another photographer snapped a picture of the girl standing in the schoolyard with a group of friends. The German press printed her name and photo. Eventually, a masked picture with her first name and the first initial of her last would turn up in the American publication *Celebrity Skin*.

The girl's family was aware that, bad as it was now, the moment she walked into the courtroom on August 9, she would have to face cameras, lights and microphones. Questions and insinuations would be thrown at her from all sides. Even though Deputy D.A. Grodin had warned them about the publicity that would ensue, no one could have predicted the actual tumult they had witnessed. Besides the local and national press, reporters from around the world thronged to the Santa Monica courthouse. London alone sent at least four reporters. Phone lines open twenty-four hours were installed to newspapers across Europe. In the face of all this attention, the mother, a friend observed, having moved against Polanski on impulse, was now "going through hell." Would the young victim have to live the rest of her life as the girl who was raped by Roman Polanski?

Both Gunson and her lawyer, Lawrence Silver, monitored the mother's growing anxieties about public confrontation. The deciding factor in the case, however, was the girl's adoptive father, himself a lawyer. He had not been consulted when his ex-wife decided to press charges against Polanski but soon became actively involved in the case. The girl's natural father and mother had divorced when she was seven, and she was subsequently adopted by her mother's second husband, the lawyer. The child and her adoptive father remained close, even after he and her mother were divorced when she was eleven. As a lawyer, he had an informed idea of what could happen to the child once she took the stand, and he was reluctant to have her testify. For a change of scenery, the girl was sent to visit him—he lived out of state—and he threatened not to send her back if there was a trial.

Lawrence Silver realized that the girl's rapid physical development would pose a major problem should she be called to testify—another reason for keeping her out of court. He watched as his client grew taller by the week. What he had first perceived as two little "bumps"—as he called them—were now "clearly identifiable breasts." This might affect a jury's attitude, particularly with Polanski sitting in the courtroom looking boyish and small. At the time of the rape, the thirteen-year-old girl was taller than her attacker; by August she would tower over him. The one hope that the prosecution had for counteracting her budding development was the set of photographs Polanski had taken, showing her appearance at the time of the rape. The prosecution would point out, however, that no matter what the girl's appearance—then or now—she had still been only thirteen, and Polanski knew it. Any other considerations were legally irrelevant.

Anjelica Huston had agreed to testify for the prosecution if the District Attorney's office would drop the drug charges against her. Gunson's case was strong. There were photos of the little girl sprawled in a Jacuzzi as she sipped champagne. There were semen-stained panties. And Huston's promised testimony. Still, Gunson wanted the girl on the stand as a willing, not a reluctant witness. Her family had now begun putting real pressure on the District Attorney's office for a plea-bargain agreement. But there was an immediate obstacle to this: the District Attorney, John Van de Kamp, had before the Polanski case made it public policy that no plea bargain be considered unless it concerned the most serious of the charges leveled against a defendant. Polanski faced very serious charges and was unwilling to plead to the most serious.

Gunson was not happy about accepting a plea bargain: he believed in his case and wanted to go to trial, provided the girl and her mother would testify. Sources close to him later said that he had wanted to drop the whole thing if the victim wouldn't take the stand. It was evident, though, that Polanski was too public a figure for this to be possible.

Both sides reluctantly pressed to win the best terms they could. In the course of plea-bargaining negotiations, Dalton twice privately repeated an offer that, as part of the rehabilitation process, Polanski would voluntarily found and fund a theater arts school for disadvantaged children, where he would also teach. "That would be a nifty place for a child molester!" grumbled a member of the prosecution team. Dalton's offer wasn't taken up.

By early August, however, a plea bargain had been arranged. On August 8, the day before the scheduled start of his trial, Polanski appeared in Santa Monica court to change his plea to guilty on a single charge, the *least* serious one of the six original counts—"unlawful sexual intercourse." He had not wanted to plead guilty to *any* of them, and even this count could result in his deportation, but Dalton had convinced him that he must compromise.

Gunson wasn't happy either. The girl's family threatened not to appear if Polanski's plea wasn't accepted, and D.A. Van de Kamp was unwilling to force the girl's return from her father's house. Gunson went into court determined that the girl's story would not be forgotten or tossed aside. He had made up his mind that Polanski would not be able to walk out of the courtroom and say afterward that he hadn't done anything. It had to be made clear that Polanski had ravished the child and had admitted it publicly. For this reason, the conditions under which Polanski's guilty plea was accepted were unusual. First, Polanski was required to enter the plea *under oath*—an unusual step—specifying precisely to *what* he pleaded guilty. Gunson wanted no ambiguity. So, after taking the oath, Polanski stood before Judge Rittenband and said, "I had sex with a female person, not my wife, under the age of 18. She was the complaining witness."

When he had finished, Gunson read Polanski a long list of questions, each of which he answered. "On March 10,

1977," asked Gunson, "the day you had intercourse with the complaining witness, how old did you believe her to be?"

"I understand she was 13," Polanski said.

"Did you *know* she was 13 years of age then?" Gunson continued.

"Yes."

Polanski also said he knew that his plea of guilty carried a possible sentence of one to fifty years in state prison and that he could be deported.

Silver, the family's lawyer, read a three-page letter to the judge expressing their wishes that the court accept Polanski's plea and their hope that he would not be incarcerated. Both Silver and the prosecution team knew that this was a calculated risk, for the letter might create a suspicion that the girl was afraid to appear publicly because she was lying. "My primary concern," said Silver, "is the present and future well-being of the girl and her family. Up to this point, the identity of my clients has been protected from public exposure." Fearful that the child would be stigmatized by the case, the family had decided that the guilty plea by the defendant was a sufficient act of contrition.

The District Attorney's office was determined that it would not appear that Polanski was getting special treatment because he was famous. Given the fact that Van de Kamp's office was accepting a plea to a lesser charge, in violation of its declared policy, a statement was issued outlining the reasons for making this exception—and making it clear that no sentencing deal had been included in the agreement to accept the plea. "Should we prosecute the defendant to the fullest degree," asked the D.A.'s office, "yet victimize the 13-year-old girl through the mass of publicity and exposure which we all know this trial would bring, and which would conceivably follow her for the rest of her life?"

In his more detailed official recommendation, Van de Kamp cited fears that scandal and publicity would further aggravate the traumatic effect the young victim had already suffered.

Before sentencing, Rittenband would have to secure various recommendations, including those of a team of psychiatrists which would be appointed to determine whether or not Polanski was "a mentally disordered sex offender." If the psychiatrists ruled that Polanski was mentally deranged, he could be committed to a state hospital for treatment and forced to register afterward as a sex offender. Once the psychiatrists' reports came in, they would be included in a comprehensive report prepared by a probation officer, a crucial factor in Rittenband's decision on the sentence.

Polanski's legal team went into plea-bargain negotiations determined about one thing: as a condition of their client's pleading guilty, they wanted a guarantee that Polanski would *not* be assigned to the female probation officer who would normally have handled the case. If Polanski was to be observed and a lengthy account written of him, they did not want a woman to do the job. The prosecution accepted this request, and the task of composing the probation report was turned over to a man named Irwin Gold.

seventeen

IN THE END, Polanski did not deny that he had had sexual intercourse with the girl. But he was angry about being accused of rape. His predilection for young girls was well known. Surely this was not the first time he had been involved with one. He felt that he was being persecuted and persecution was a nightmare he had done nothing special to deserve. But no matter how well developed they are physically or how available, the very young are legally off limits in our society. Although the age guidelines vary from state to state, an underage child cannot consent to perform sexual acts, for she cannot make decisions with the authority of an adult. (Even the merchandising of the very young in fashion and film does not change this.)

Since the probation report would affect his fate, Polanski worked on his probation officer, Irwin Gold, for whom he painted a picture of a tragic past, a compliant girl, and remorse for anything he might have done wrong. Polanski had stepped in front of a camera before and knew how to act a part. As the probation report shows, he managed to win Gold's sympathy—as well as that of the court-appointed psychiatrists. It is a testimonial to Polanski's ability to manipulate a situation that the probation report was so favorable to him.

Gold began with a capsule narrative of Polanski's troubled life, sketching wartime Poland, self-imposed exile from communism, and the Manson murders. Mention of two head injuries—in the Cracow bunker and in an automobile accident—led Gold to comment:

> Although defendant has been under abnormal periods of stress throughout his life, he has never sought psychiatric or other professional assistance, implying that any psychiatric care could, conceivably, interfere with the creative process.

181

After detailing the allegations, the report moved to Polanski's confession. Now, for the first time, Polanski offered *his* version of what had happened on Mulholland Drive, stressing the thirteen-year-old's initiative. More than just a compliant partner, the child was almost a seductress. In Polanski's narrative, she began to assume control in the car:

> She mentioned that she liked champagne. . . . She once got drunk at her father's house. . . . She talked about sex. . . . She said she first had sex at eight with a kid down the street and later her boyfriend.

Inside Nicholson's house, the little girl had taken "her blouse off." Although he didn't mention the child's being groggy with alcohol and drugs, he suggested that he had been worried about his own condition. Having been drinking, he now claimed, he feared taking a Quaalude. He denied any "actual offer" of drugs to the girl but did corroborate her having claimed to be asthmatic when he wanted to enter the pool with her. The faked asthma attack posed a problem for Polanski's story, since he claimed the child had been a "willing" partner, so he quickly cut away from it:

> I heard a car coming. I was apprehensive. Some maniacs used to come to the compound.

This veiled allusion to his own prior victimization preceded the point in the story where he "told her to rest in the bedroom." The montage of the "maniacs" and the bedroom scene made Polanski a more sympathetic character. As to what went on inside the bedroom, he was strategically laconic:

> I went to the bedroom. She never objected.

The sole information offered is that he "withdrew before climax," another well-calculated detail. What happened between her consent and his withdrawal was simple:

> The whole thing was very spontaneous. It was not planned.

The girl had told a different story to the grand jury, to the district attorneys, and even to Gold—but from this mo-

ment, it was Polanski's version that would determine the
probation officer's conclusions. A groggy thirteen-year-old
who didn't know the word "sodomy" was no match for this
brilliant actor, director and screenwriter. Gold wrote:

> During the subsequent interview with the defendant he
> expressed great remorse regarding any possible effect the
> present offense might have had upon the victim. He ex-
> pressed great pity and compassion for her, stating that he
> knew the legal proceedings have been extremely diffi-
> cult for her. He stated that because of the many tragedies
> that he, himself, has known in his own life he feels great
> empathy for a young person in distress.

This passage registered events not explicit in it: the impassioned exchange between Gold and Polanski as the defendant recounted how often he had been kicked in life.
"Haven't *you* kicked someone, Roman?" asked Gold—at
which Polanski broke down and wept. This moment,
sources indicate, was the turning point for the probation
officer, who became unusually involved in the case, fascinated by the possibility of comprehending and socializing
Roman Polanski as no one had done before.

In the course of the "mentally disordered sex offender"
proceedings, Polanski became the object of psychiatric
scrutiny and was deemed to be neither mentally ill nor
sexually deviant. One psychiatrist even remarked on Polanski's "good judgement"—an odd assessment in a rape case.
Accepting Polanski's account, as Gold had, the psychiatrist
characterized the offense as "an isolated instance of tran-
sient poor judgement and loss of normal inhibitions in circumstances of intimacy and collaboration in creative
work." Compassionate with regard to Polanski, the psychiatrist scored the mother's "permissiveness and knowledge
of circumstances." Even the rape victim herself was called
to account for her "physical maturity and willingness and
provocativeness," as if the child were to be blamed for her
physical appearance, her natural endowments. In this light,
the psychiatrist commended Polanski for his "lack of coer-
cion" as well as for "his solicitude concerning pregnancy."
He felt that Polanski was unlikely to "reoffend" and saw no
need for psychiatric treatment. Moreover, he expressed

concern about the possible effects any time in prison might have on someone of such "highly sensitive personality and devotion to his work." Another psychiatrist suggested that Polanski would benefit from therapy—"not for a sexual problem but for unresolved depression." This psychiatrist also concluded that "the present offense was neither a forceful nor aggressive sexual act."

Finally, Gold concluded his findings with all the authority of an observer sanctioned by law to interpret what he had seen. He recommended probation, on the basis of Polanski's assertion "that the act was not premeditated, that it was spontaneous." He noted that Polanski felt "sincere remorse" and that he was a foreigner with different "manners and mores." Despite a turbulent past, Gold noted, Polanski "has not only survived, he has prevailed." Polanski's momentary "poor judgement" was cited, but also his commendable "solicitude" about the possibility of pregnancy. Gold wrote:

> It is believed that incalculable emotional damage could result from incarcerating the defendant whose own life has been a seemingly unending series of punishments.

This was the victimizer as victim—a role Polanski had played to the hilt.

Despite these recommendations, Judge Rittenband was against probation for Polanski. Having once stated that "sometimes trying to diagnose a psychiatric condition is like trying to get a black cat on a dark night, in a coal cellar," Rittenband didn't place much stock in the psychiatric reports—and thought the entire probation report the worst "whitewash" he had ever seen. If Gold and the psychiatrists had been convinced by Polanski, Rittenband hadn't come close.

On September 16, Rittenband called the principals in the case to his chambers. There he laid out his decision, which would be announced publicly on the nineteenth. He informed Defense Attorney Dalton, Prosecutor Gunson and Probation Officer Gold that he planned to send Polanski to the State Facility at Chino for ninety days, ostensibly for more extensive diagnosis, but in fact, the judge intimated he would consider this as the defendant's entire punishment. Both Gunson and Gold objected, reminding the judge that Chino was supposed to be used solely for diagnostic purposes, not punishment. Rittenband refused to be swayed, insisting that Polanski would be safer at the state prison than in county jail. At this point the central—but unspoken—issue in the case wasn't jail but *deportation*. This was what Dalton had fought to avoid and what the judge seemed increasingly determined to ensure. If Rittenband couldn't deport Polanski—that was the province of the Department of Immigration and Naturalization—he *could* make deportation virtually inevitable. A term in state prison rather than the county jail would help provide a sufficient ground on which the Immigration authorities could move.

Rittenband told Dalton that he would grant a ninety-day stay to allow Polanski to complete *Hurricane*. He was unwilling to announce a longer stay, because of what the press and public reaction would inevitably be, but—instructing all present to keep quiet about it—the judge said that he would be willing to come back to court at the end of the first ninety days and grant additional time. Finally, steamrolling on, Rittenband issued a set of instructions for the court session on the nineteenth. Dalton was to argue for probation; Gunson was to ask for imprisonment. Then Rittenband would rule, sending Polanski to Chino for "diagnosis."

On September 19, Dalton rose in court and addressed Rittenband. He stressed two points. First he contended that rather than gaining Polanski preferential treatment, his celebrity was leading to his being treated with "extra animus." Far from asking for special treatment, Dalton said he merely wanted to ensure that his client would be accorded the same treatment any ordinary defendant would receive. Dalton attempted to limit the consideration of the court to the single charge of unlawful sexual intercourse—one which he tried to make seem as benign as possible. Painfully trying to differentiate unlawful sexual intercourse from rape, he remarked that "this particular offense doesn't have the connotation of rape"—a misleading contention if one examines the California Criminal Law, in which the two are explicitly linked.

Conscious of the threat of deportation, Dalton stated that he wished to "remind" the court that "this is not a crime that is *malum in se*" (evil in itself). Whether or not a crime is *malum in se* is one of the criteria for determining whether moral turpitude is involved, and if Polanski was convicted of a crime of moral turpitude, he would be immediately subject to *deportation*.

Having cited the probation and psychiatric reports, Dalton asserted that Polanski "is a criminal only by accident; that there are many complex social and psychological factors that were involved in this situational event which otherwise was a complete departure from his normal mode of conduct." Avoiding mention of alcohol or Quaaludes, the defense suggested the child's consent. By denying that unlawful sexual intercourse was rape, Dalton implied that the difference involved consent.

Next to address the court, Prosecutor Gunson strenuously objected to Dalton's remarks. While not reminding the defense that consent in a case involving an underage child is immaterial, Gunson recalled that there had been factors that would have rendered consent difficult if not impossible—the champagne and the Quaaludes. Gunson said that he had been particularly disturbed by the implication in both the probation report and the psychiatric evaluations that "the sexual activities occurred naturally and mutually." Testimony offered by the girl to the Grand Jury had indicated otherwise. Gunson argued that far from being an unfortunate accident, there were signs "that this is more than a normal course of action, a situational event. It appears that it was almost planned." Thus Gunson urged that the defendant be sentenced to time in custody.

Having heard Dalton and Gunson state their positions for the public record, Rittenband was ready to rule.

Although the prosecutrix was not an inexperienced girl, this of course is not a license to the defendant, a man of the world, in his forties, to engage in an act of unlawful sexual intercourse with her. The law was designed for the protection of females under the age of eighteen years, and it is no defense to such a charge that the female might not have resisted the act.

As indicated in advance, Rittenband ordered Polanski to Chino for ninety days of diagnostic testing, and at Dalton's request, a ninety-day stay was granted, allowing Polanski to continue work on *Hurricane* before reporting to prison.

When Polanski left the courtroom, major misunderstandings remained. What was the purpose of the stay at Chino and its relation to the final sentence? The judge had privately agreed that the only time Polanski would have to serve was that required for the diagnostic study—however long that took to complete. This was what Dalton assured Polanski. But Rittenband expected the diagnostic study to last the full ninety days, and if it didn't, he would insist that any remaining time be served.

Although Rittenband granted a stay so that Polanski could work on his new film, the judge had been disturbed because the director had signed the contract to direct *Hurricane*, implying confidence on his part that he would get off scot-free or at worst be given probation. Now Rittenband grew increasingly agitated by what he perceived as Polanski's blasé public demeanor. The arrival of then sixteen-year-old Nastassia Kinski to visit Polanski infuriated the judge, despite the director's claim that she was there for professional reasons and had brought her mother as chaperone. To the judge, this man facing rape charges was acting in a contemptuous manner by publicly flaunting his relationship with yet another teenager.

But the decisive provocation came just ten days after the sentencing hearing when the Santa Monica *Evening Outlook* published a photograph of Polanski in Munich, seated with several lovely women at a table covered with beer steins. The caption read:

> Movie director Roman Polanski puffs a cigar as he enjoys companionship of young ladies during a visit 9/28 to the Munich Oktoberfest, world's largest beer festival. Sources say Polanski came to Bavaria's capital as a tourist and just wants to relax. A Santa Monica court ordered Polanski to undergo a 90-day diagnostic study at a state prison but permitted him to finish a film first.

Enraged, Rittenband announced that he was going to send Polanski to jail immediately. Dalton was asked to get

Polanski back to Santa Monica for a hearing on October 21. But Polanski had already left Munich for Tahiti, where an airline strike caused him to miss the court date in California. The hearing was rescheduled, and on October 24, Polanski and his producer, Dino De Laurentiis, informed the court that the director had been in Munich on business. De Laurentiis said that he had been unable to visit the German distributor himself and had asked Polanski to represent him. At the hearing, Polanski was also questioned about Nastassia Kinski. He claimed that although she had visited him in California and Munich, it had always been in the company of a chaperone. Finally, Rittenband agreed to permit Polanski to remain free, but it was obvious he would grant no further stays as originally indicated. In chambers, he said he didn't really believe De Laurentiis, who seemed only to be trying to cover for Polanski.

Polanski was due to report to Chino on December 19, but to avoid the crush of reporters, the court permitted him to arrive three days early. The night before he left, a group of friends, including Kenneth Tynan and Jack Nicholson, gave Polanski a going-away party. He was understandably depressed and ill-tempered, anxious about prison and the possibility of being raped himself because of his small size.

The diagnostic tests took forty-two days to complete, during which Polanski was incarcerated with fellow inmates whom he described as "the scum of society." Meanwhile, De Laurentiis announced that Polanski wouldn't be directing *Hurricane*. His status was too uncertain to be bankable.

On January 27, Polanski was released from prison. Badly shaken by the experience, he left assuming that at least he had now completed all the time he would have to serve behind bars. But on January 30, Rittenband called Gunson and Dalton to his chambers in preparation for final sentencing on February 1, and informed them that it was his intention to send Polanski back to prison for an additional forty-eight days—to make his incarceration total ninety days. Worse still, Rittenband indicated that he would consent to the forty-eight day limit *only* if Polanski would agree to deport himself voluntarily upon release. Otherwise, he would leave him in jail.

There was a second meeting the following day. By now, even Gunson was in disaccord with the judge, arguing that Rittenband should sentence Polanski to ninety days in the county jail—with credit for time already served—rather than send him to state prison if he insisted on the additional forty-eight days. The judge refused, as Dalton later recalled, arguing that "the appearance of a state prison sentence must be maintained for the press." Gunson felt that, hard as he had fought for time in prison for Polanski, a commitment had been made to the defendant for one sort of sentence and that it should be kept. But nothing swayed Rittenband, determined to force Polanski's deportation.

Apprised of Rittenband's decision, Polanski drove to the Los Angeles airport and booked the last remaining seat, a first-class ticket, on British Airways flight #598 to London, which departed at 5:57 P.M., arriving in London the next morning at 11:40 London time. Due in Rittenband's courtroom that day, Polanski called Dalton and said not to expect him there. He had had enough. Why serve additional time if he was going to be deported anyway?

At first the press concentrated on trying to figure out exactly how Polanski had managed to get away. But there had hardly been an elaborate escape plan, for Polanski had never been deprived of his passport. Since his arrest, he had been free to enter and leave the country. The counter agents at British Airways thought nothing of Polanski's ticket purchase since he had flown with them several times since the rape case began.

In London, after lunch with his friend Nigel Politzer, at which he complained bitterly about having been locked up with murderers and other lowlifes, Polanski met with a lawyer, who informed him that he could be extradited from England and had better leave at once. In France, as a naturalized citizen, he would be protected from extradition on the charges for which he had been arrested. So he flew to Paris and secluded himself in the apartment he kept on Avenue Montaigne.

Back in Los Angeles, Rittenband issued a bench warrant for Polanski's arrest in the United States. In addition, a move was made for international extradition should Polanski turn up in a country where this would apply. L.A.'s

Chief Deputy District Attorney Stephen Trott was quoted in the Los Angeles *Herald Examiner* as saying, "We will extradite Polanski from anywhere, as long as there's a treaty. . . . We've got the dogs out. The hounds are on his trail."

On February 1, Rittenband agreed to postpone Polanski's sentencing to February 14, to allow Dalton to attempt to persuade his client to return voluntarily. But within twenty-four hours, the judge had changed his mind and wanted to sentence Polanski *in absentia*. Rittenband was agitated about possible public reaction to two things. First, Gold had revealed to the press that the psychiatric reports from Chino had been favorable to Polanski and that, like the first psychiatrists in the case, they recommended that Polanski not spend further time in jail. Second, Roger Gunson announced that Rittenband had planned to give Polanski additional time in jail when he sentenced him on February 1.

In Paris, Polanski talked to his old friend Michael Klinger on the telephone about the possibility of holding a press conference. "Nobody's heard my side of the story," he complained. "Roman," Klinger snapped, "you're out of your mind, you know!" But Polanski was insistent. "Roman," Klinger went on, "don't mistake this for one of your film press conferences. If you go out in front of the press, they're going to crucify you. They're going to be finished with all of your smart-assed tactics. They'll kill you! This isn't someone saying whether you shot the right angle, you know."

Polanski didn't go through with the press conference. On February 6, Rittenband spoke to reporters about the case, stating that, because of his crime of moral turpitude, Polanski didn't belong in America. Calling Rittenband's remarks "incredible," on February 14 Dalton moved that Rittenband be disqualified "because of bias and prejudice and a fair and impartial hearing may not be held before him." A few days later the judge responded, denying that he was or had been biased or prejudiced against Polanski, but he agreed to permit the case to be reassigned to another judge. No judge was named to replace Rittenband, and the Polanski case was removed from the court calendar. No sentencing would take place until Polanski returned—something he didn't seem about to do.

Months after Polanski's flight, when the question of his possible return was raised with the U.S. Department of Immigration, an officer pointed out that Polanski's return was no longer entirely up to him—even if he were willing to serve additional time in prison. As a foreign national who had pleaded guilty to a felony charge, now that he was outside the country, he could be denied a visa should he attempt to return.

eighteen

BARRED FROM returning to Hollywood, Polanski decided to make a Hollywood-style extravaganza in Europe, an adaptation of Thomas Hardy's *Tess of the d'Urbervilles.* He had read it a decade before when the role of Tess had been proposed to Sharon Tate. The book had made him cry, so vivid was the portrait of its defiled heroine. Now, tormented by his own rape case, Polanski remembered the novel and decided to script and direct it, with seventeen-year-old Nastassia Kinski starring.

It was her mother who had introduced Nastassia Kinski to Polanski. At the age of fifteen, Nastassia became Polanski's lover. Polanski gave her books to read and suggested ways for developing her acting abilities, including a short stint with Lee Strasberg. Kinski's acting career had begun at thirteen, when she appeared in New German director Wim Wenders' *The Wrong Move.* Later she frolicked in the buff with Marcello Mastroianni in an Italian picture, Alberto Lattuada's *Stay as You Are,* nude stills from which appeared in *Playboy.* Polanski thought Kinski the perfect Tess because of what he saw as her vulnerability.

Seeking money to embark on the project, Polanski discussed it with his old friend Claude Berri, the French director-producer who had recently made *One Wild Moment,* about a middle-aged father who has an affair with his best friend's daughter. Berri figured that, as a costume film, *Tess* would be expensive to make—more so because Polanski feared extradition if he went to England, and Hardy's Wessex, based on nineteenth-century Dorset, would have to be painstakingly replicated in France. Moreover, it seemed to Berri that the film could work *only* if the proper Tess was cast. Late one night Berri was finally persuaded to produce the film when Polanski turned up at his home with Kinski: ". . . seeing her in her skirt and little blouse," Berri told

L'Express, "I understood that I was going to accept." By March 1978, a bit more than a month after fleeing Los Angeles, Polanski had secured Berri's agreement to back the film.

Tess was too costly a proposition for his own company, RENN Productions, to bankroll alone, so Berri acquired a coproducer, Timothy Burrill of Burrill Productions in England (who had earlier been an associate producer on *Macbeth*) and additional backing from the Société Française de Production in France. Although being made in France, *Tess* would be an international film, shot in English.

Film rights to the novel were held by the estate of David Selznick, who had purchased them in the hope of making the film with his wife Jennifer Jones. He had envisioned an extravaganza of the magnitude of his *Gone with the Wind.* The project was never realized, however, but the rights would not go into the public domain again until January 1979, ten months away. Wanting to immerse himself in work in order to counter the discomfort of his notoriety, Polanski was impatient. The now enthusiastic Berri was persuaded to pay sixty thousand dollars in order to secure the rights immediately. As a bonus, Selznick's son gave Polanski and Berri one hundred pages of his father's notes on the film. With two collaborators, Gerard Brach and Dorset-resident John Brownjohn, Polanski set to work writing a script, shortening Hardy's title to *Tess,* and dedicating the film to his late wife.

Nastassia Kinski was packed off to England in April for four months of work with a speech coach to perfect a credible Dorset accent and to learn the gestures and mannerisms of a genuine English farmgirl.

By July 31, Polanski was ready to begin shooting, first on location along the Normandy coast and later in the studio. He had spared no expense. Obsessed with precise detail as usual, Polanski insisted upon accurate period costumes and settings. A special breed of English chickens was imported, rustic country lanes created, and telephone wires were run underground to obliterate all traces of the twentieth century. A scale reproduction of Stonehenge was constructed for the film's final scene.

For Polanski, the making of *Tess* was a trying period, in

which the originally slated twenty-two weeks of shooting dragged into nine months—two of them lost to strikes—and the film became the most expensive ever produced in France—costing eleven million dollars. During shooting, Polanski's cinematographer Geoffrey Unsworth—who had worked on *2,001: A Space Odyssey, Cabaret,* and *Superman*—suffered a heart attack and died: a major disaster for the production, as a new cinematographer, Ghislain Cloquet, had to be brought in immediately. Polanski later described the unenviable position in which Cloquet found himself: "We didn't even stop the shooting. I thought . . . that it was necessary to continue. . . . The day after his [Unsworth's] death, when we arrived on the stage, there was this bizarre atmosphere, this emptiness, as if everyone hadn't yet arrived, as if a large part of the crew were missing." Cloquet carefully studied Unsworth's completed material, talked to the technicians who had been working with him, and managed to adjust to the precedent of Unsworth's distinctive pictorial style.

Because Polanski couldn't work in Hollywood, his career and reputation were staked on *Tess.* Since Klinger had dissuaded him from giving a press conference after his flight to Paris, Polanski had restrained himself from commenting publicly on the rape. Still, he was itching to have his say, and when Jerzy Kosinski suggested he give an interview to Mike Wallace on TV's "60 Minutes," he agreed. Wallace brought cameras and crew to a location outside Cherbourg, where they filmed Polanski filming. First America watched Polanski instruct Nastassia Kinski on doing repeated pushups so that her arms would really tremble for a scene. Then, Wallace asked the big question: "Why did you get involved with a thirteen-year-old-girl?" "Since the girl is anonymous," Polanski replied, "and I hope for her sake that she will be, I would like to describe her to you. She is not a child, she is a young woman. She had, and she testified to it, previous sexual experience. She wasn't unschooled in sexual matters. She was consenting and willing. Whatever I did was wrong. I think I paid for it. I went through a year of incredible hardship, and I think I paid for it."

Even some of Polanski's friends were appalled by his

performance. Kosinski describes Polanski as "situational," that is, frequently unable to comprehend the implications of actions, to see beyond the immediate situation. Kosinski, who also appeared on the program, was shocked when Polanski defended himself by arguing the girl's complicity, even though it was legally irrelevant. When Kosinski called him afterward in France, Polanski seemed proud of himself:

"Wasn't the program great?" he asked.

"Romek," Kosinski said, "why did you talk about that? You said that she wasn't a child."

"Well, she wasn't."

"Well, actually, she *was*."

"She wasn't!" Polanski insisted. "I know that!"

"No, Romek, when you were fourteen, you were a child."

"Yes, well, yes," Polanski stammered, "but, you know, in terms of everything else."

"No," Kosinski retorted, "this is not the issue, 'in terms of everything else.' In terms of everything else, that's not the point. The point is that we talk about it because she *was* a child. Otherwise there would be no issue. Had she been twenty-seven or seventy-five, there would be no program. Why did you talk about that?"

"Well," said Polanski, "I had to talk about *something*."

In another of the rare interviews Polanski granted at the time, the journalist cited the case of a judge who had argued that women can be at fault in rape cases when they wear outfits that provoke the attacker. "Let me stop you," interrupted Polanski, "because I don't want to be quoted in all that context that you evoke now. It does me only harm." But for someone who wanted to be treated seriously —as a filmmaker and artist—*this* interview was another wrong move, since it was published in the raunchy magazine *Club*, where Polanski's comments and photo appeared opposite pictures of glassy-eyed women removing their blouses, with the headline: "Experts Say . . . You Really Can Get Girls Through Hypnotism!" This was another example of Polanski's "situational" behavior. How else could he have failed to see the implications of appearing in this context?

In a situation, however, Polanski's feelings of persecution—real and imagined—could make him alert to the slightest threat. To friends, he seemed to be constantly on the watch. One night he was dining in Paris with a well-known American actor. When a drunk approached their table and began to pester them, Polanski promptly told him to get lost. The drunk left in a huff, and Polanski and the actor resumed dinner, remaining at their table for another hour. As they left the restaurant, the drunk suddenly appeared with a knife and addressed Polanski, who whirled around and hit him in the face with a heavy crystal ash tray he had surreptitiously concealed in his pocket for protection. Polanski's actor friend had forgotten about the drunk, but he hadn't, and expected something like this to occur. Discovering that he had broken the man's jaw, Polanski coolly called an ambulance.

When Polanski finished shooting *Tess* at the end of April 1979, he decided to edit it as a long film to achieve a rhythm and style appropriate to his conception of the material. Because the film had been so costly to shoot, this decision involved a big gamble: long films are difficult to sustain and sell. In May the nervous producers ordered Polanski and Kinski to Cannes to pre-sell *Tess*. Their arrival was announced with the maximum publicity, but when they appeared together in a virtual brawl of a press conference, reporters had little interest in talking about *Tess*—which was still in production. Polanski grew hostile when queried about his relations with Kinski. A fracas broke out when someone from the audience shouted at Polanski, "Don't bother to come back to America! We already have enough problems!" Finally, Polanski and Kinski ducked out as the audience laughed and jeered.

Tess opened in France on October 31, 1979, but it wasn't until almost nine months later that American audiences saw it. Distributors feared that a film this long (three hours plus an intermission) wouldn't go over commercially. Moreover, because of the rape case, Polanski was widely thought to be too much of a commercial risk.

Frustrated at the temporary inability to sell *Tess* in America, Polanski talked about Hollywood with Polish actor Daniel Olbrychski, then on his way to the Academy Awards ceremony, where his new picture, *The Tin Drum*, was up for a prize. In adapting Günter Grass's novel about Oscar, a bizarre little boy who doesn't grow, German director Volker Schlöndorff had originally toyed with the idea of using the then forty-four-year-old Polanski as the child.

After discussing the film with Olbrychski, Polanski switched to the actor's trip to Hollywood. In public he had been adopting a posture of remorse and contrition for his actions in California, but now he was talking privately. "You want her name and number?" he cackled in a high-pitched, loud shriek.

"Whose?" asked Olbrychski.

"She'd be sixteen by now," Polanski continued. "I'll give you her name and number. *That* would be the Polish revenge!"

In the press, Polanski began to hint that he planned to return to the States. Actually, the decision wasn't his alone, since Immigration authorities had the option of refusing him a visa because of his crime, even if he planned to surrender. With this in mind, a thick immigration file was maintained on him, to be considered in case he applied for a visa. That Polanski wasn't wanted any longer by the U.S. was suggested when he found he could travel freely outside France with no attempt to extradite him being initiated.

In February of 1980, *Tess* won three Cesars—the French academy awards. The film was named best picture of 1980, Polanski was voted best director, and it also garnered the award for cinematography for Geoffrey Unsworth and Ghislain Cloquet. *Tess* was invited to be screened at numerous festivals, and Polanski traveled widely, promoting it.

As part of a group of French filmmakers, Polanski and Kinski—whose romance was long over, but who remained good friends—flew to Argentina for a festival there. When the group visited the enormous ranch of a fabulously wealthy Argentinian, Nastassia Kinski removed her clothes, marched out to the pool, and stretched out stark naked in the sun, to the shock of the proper Latin ladies gathered there—and the wide-eyed delight of the polo ponies' grooms who broke into giggles as the girl began slapping and swatting at the mosquitoes who were nibbling her all over. Lunch was served at a large table where the hosts and their French guests appeared in elegant attire. Having put her clothes back on, Kinski raised a bare foot onto her chair and sat with her knee folded up before the tabletop. "Look at the way she eats," whispered one of the ladies, "like a ravenous puppy dog!" Polanski hadn't returned from jogging when lunch began and showed up midway, perspiration dripping from his face, still wearing a sweat-stained jogging suit. Without a word, he sat down and grabbed a linen napkin, reaching under his sweatshirt to wipe the perspiration from his neck and underarms. This was the old Romek calculating his shock effects. Finally, he regaled his hosts with a story about a trip he had once made to Thailand to make a sex film on a lean eighteen-thousand-dollar budget. But the actors he hired "couldn't get it up," he said, no matter what aphrodisiacs he plied them with.

Back in Paris, Polanski learned that Columbia Pictures —which had earlier turned down the film—had agreed to distribute *Tess* in the United States. When it opened there, Polanski's long shot paid off, with the film receiving even better reviews than it had in France. *Tess* was an unexpected box office hit, and stacked up choice critical awards and won three Oscars. What everyone seemed most delighted by was Polanski's newfound erotic discretion in *Tess*. In a rave review in the New York *Daily News*, Kathleen Carroll summed it up: "Roman Polanski's movies tend to be as bizarre and shocking as his own troubled personal life. Now along comes Polanski's *Tess*, a three-hour movie that has been directed with such admirable restraint it reminds one of some of the gently civil romantic epics of the past—of the more genteel work of directors like David Lean and Vincente Minnelli. Polanski is obviously anxious to change his image as a director if nothing else." A more telling assessment was offered by Peter Ackroyd, in the *Spectator*, when *Tess* opened in London: "In all the romantic images of this film—the moon breaking through the massed clouds, the enchanted forests, the scenes of mourning and rejoicing seen from a distance—we have the unstated presence of an infantile sexuality: infinitely suggestible but fragile, soft but somehow lurid."

Like *Macbeth*, *Tess* is an adaptation of a classic to which Polanski was drawn in troubled times by its rigorous structure, its three-dimensional characters and its relevance to his recent experiences. But in *Macbeth*, Polanski chose to show *all*—including violence and nudity absent from the play. *Tess* is different, with its strategy of exclusion and reticence. Alec's murder, for instance, takes place off screen, in a space only imagined, not seen. The act is indicated by two synecdochic devices—blood dripping from the floor of Alec's room to the ceiling below and a red stain at the edge of Tess's skirt.

The film's central scene—less a rape than a seduction— is obscured by a thick haze. Like the shorts Polanski conceived for *Oh! Calcutta!*, *Tess* represents a sexual act that is never fully disclosed, only hinted at. In a cinematic paradox, the act takes place within the frame of the screen, but remains hidden, like the monstrous child in *Rosemary's Baby.*

The motif of looking is especially important in *Tess*, whose opening scene offers a group of teenaged girls to the delighted view of Angel Clare. Stopping to watch as they dance in the field, Angel spots Tess, but no words are exchanged, just glances. Like the story, Angel must move on, despite the temptation of dancing with the girls in white— and looking at Tess. Throughout the film, shots of her slow down the story, making it languid, even static. Without them, *Tess* wouldn't last its unusual running time. At every possible opportunity, Polanski's camera explores Kinski's beauty, as the wind ruffles her thick hair and she poses against the backdrop of horizon, sun and sky. Sometimes a close-up of Tess can afford a kind of silent soliloquy, as anticipation or pain are registered upon the contours of her face. More often, these shots convey little or no narrative information. The camera is held upon her, and the action seems suspended in the frozen tableau, the perfect pictorial composition. When she is sent by her parents to "claim kin" with the wealthy d'Urberville family, the trip is signified by a shot of Tess in the carriage. Other filmmakers might quickly cut away, but Polanski holds the shot, long after it has ceased to *mean* anything. The journey completed, there is another shot of Tess—walking this time.

Ironically, even though both shots signify a journey, they don't hasten the action, but slow it down. A more likely procedure would be to get Tess to her destination as quickly as possible, using temporal ellipses to cut the kind of slack time Polanski leaves in.

Clearly, it isn't ineptitude that leads Polanski to drag out his story. One ellipsis, for example, demonstrates unusual narrative mastery: after Tess returns to her family, having been ravished by Alec d'Urberville, she is seen working in the fields. The laborers sit for lunch, and as she slices a loaf of bread, crying is heard from off screen. When a baby is brought to Tess and she opens her blouse to breast-feed it, two important facts are conveyed: she has given birth and at least nine months have passed since the last shot. Not actually shown, the time signified by the gap between shots is vividly indicated. With this kind of storytelling skill, why would Polanski spend so much time on long-held shots of Tess that don't advance the action?

A clue is to be found in the explicit eroticization of certain shots of her by ascribing them to, say, Alec's point of view. For example, Tess is seen attempting to learn to whistle to entertain Mrs. d'Urberville's birds. She purses her lips and blows, but to no avail. After a few moments of this, a whistled tune is heard coming from off screen. Alec, it seems, has been watching her all along from the grass, his angle of vision identified with the camera's. Only now does it become perceptible that the shot of Tess was from a low angle—and *why*.

This kind of point-of-view shot, in which the observation of Tess is identified with a character's gaze, naturalizes the presence of the camera. But even when someone isn't looking, the camera is, suggesting the voyeurism implicit in the cinematic scrutiny of woman. The objectification of a woman, her enactment of scenes for a faceless director and his anonymous audience isn't unique to Polanski. But with its endless views of Kinski, *Tess is* an extreme case. Now, it might be objected that in *Tess* women also spy on men, as in the scene where the lovesick milkmaids watch Angel Clare from a window. But whereas the male gaze—Alec's or Angel's—is always active, the women remain passive: in the next shot, they nearly swoon as Angel carries each of them across a puddle so that they won't muddy their Sunday finery. And he only does it to get the chance to carry Tess, the one *he* has chosen.

"If you're wise," Alec d'Urberville tells Tess, "you'll let the world get a clearer sight of that beauty." In Polanski's world this isn't bad advice.

Polanski is fascinated by Tess's character, he told *Le Monde*, for the way in which she responds to her humiliations with dignity and integrity. Rebellion, Polanski feels, is something Tess can't consider. Having just been inspected and questioned, himself, Polanski switched positions again, assuming the dominant role of interrogator, using the camera to record Tess's responses. This impassioned scrutiny is as much the subject of the film as anything that happens in it—adding a cinematic dimension to Hardy's novel. In *Tess*, the voyeuristic—and sadistic—impulses of a student short like *Break Up the Ball* are motivated within a fully developed narrative context.

Anxious to get his career going again, to put recent troubles behind him, Polanski made a film about *precisely* the topic he wished to avoid—rape. "Ugliness is in the eye of the beholder," he told those who saw parallels to the California rape case. This audacious tactic follows the logic of Mosquito—the character Polanski played in *What?*—who provokes sexual innuendos about himself, then lashes out when they're made.

There is much talk of confession in *Tess*, the revelation of past sins. But as Polanski's confession, *Tess* offers the rapist's view of rape. Tess is sent to the d'Urberville estate because of her mother's ambitions. The mother encourages her daughter into Alec's arms: "So you charmed them after all, didn't you?" the woman rejoices when Tess returns from a first meeting with Alec with an offer of employment. "Our Tess is going to be a lady!" And when Tess later wants to go back to her family, Alec says, "At least let me drive you home," much as Polanski had done with the girl from Woodland Hills. Even the choice of Kinski to play Tess was significant with regard to the rape: Polanski said he associated Kinski with the rape case since he had been given the assignment by *Vogue Hommes* because of the photos of her in the issue of the French *Vogue* he had guest-edited.

In light of Polanski's then-recent troubles, it is significant that Alec isn't really menacing but a gentle seducer who tries to make Tess feel sorry for him, telling her he's been "in torment" since her arrival. "Tess, I'm dying for you," he implores, as they ride together through the misty and romantic wilderness. Alec doesn't seem to force Tess: his strategy is psychological, not physical. As they copulate, all harsh and brutal details are misted over. When Polanski depicted a rape in *Rosemary's Baby*, the National Catholic Office for Motion Pictures condemned the film. But *Tess*— Polanski's confession—was named one of the "top ten" features for 1980 by the Catholic Conference. Throughout *Tess*, the rapist isn't really distinguishable from her lover and husband, the idealistic Angel Clare. Although Leigh Lawson (Alec) and Peter Firth (Angel) look nothing alike, they're easily confused here.

The most curious detail in the rape sequence is that it is Tess who first does violence to Alec, pushing him from the horse, so that he topples to the ground: his head bloodied when it hits a stone. For a moment, victim and victimizer shift roles. He ravishes her only after she expresses sorrow at what she's done *to him*. Emblem of Alec's status as victim, the head wound—not in the novel—has obvious personal associations for Polanski. "I see a lot of Roman in Tess," Kinski has said. "He is very much like her." The reciprocity between victim and victimizer, explored in Polanski's work as early as *The Fat and the Lean*, is given its fullest expression in *Tess*. Polanski identifies with Tess because she's a victim of society's mores—much as he perceived himself to have been in the rape case. Polanski's *Tess* shows the victimizer as victim. No wonder he admires the dignity with which Tess responds to humiliation.

Tess is dedicated to Sharon Tate ostensibly because she first recommended Hardy's novel to him. A more cynical view would see the dedication as a play for sympathy, a reference to past victimization. More than that, Tess is *like* Sharon was—or as Polanski saw her—passive, childish, compliant. The static shots of Tess that slow down the film's story are like nothing so much as stills of the sort Polanski took of Sharon Tate for *Playboy*—scenes of desire. In *Tess*, Polanski might have identified with the victim— but he was also her victimizer, hidden behind the staring camera. For a long time, Roman Polanski has known what it's like on both sides, in both roles.

epilogue

WITH *Rosemary's Baby* and *Chinatown, Tess* is among the most polished of Polanski's films. Though personal reverberations are there, they are tempered by the imperatives of conventional, commercial narrative. In short, although made outside Hollywood, *Tess* is a Hollywood film. Polanski reveals himself more directly—if painfully—in rougher, less acclaimed movies such as *What?* and *The Tenant*, playing himself or his avatars as he did in early acting roles.

In *What?*, the outrageous and contradictory impulses of the aggressive, obnoxious Mosquito suggest the public Polanski, swapping jibes with the press, whether in Los Angeles, Warsaw or Cannes. The caricature indicates a rare ironic self-knowledge absent from his public demeanor. Why, one wonders, if he sees himself and his image *this* clearly, does he persist in his often hostile relations with press and public?

Polanski's most compelling attempt at self-scrutiny thus far—and arguably his best film—is *The Tenant*, whose intimate iconography is rivaled only by Jean Cocteau at his most personal. *The Tenant* is Polanski's *Blood of a Poet*, his portrait of the artist as a suicide. In both Polanski and Cocteau, the symbolic suicide occurs in a theatricalized space: jutting from a building's façade, balconies hold applauding spectators, as if the self-destruction were a show—a bitter commentary on the artist's public performance.

The Cocteau-mask in *Blood of a Poet* has its counterpart in *The Tenant*, in which we are offered a Polanski-mask and a hint of what lies behind. When the Polanski-mask and jester's cap are forcibly placed on the little girl, who cries out in his voice, this, one realizes, is another ironic self-portrait—a revelation of the tiny, victimized child.

Once, years ago, Romek drew himself as a wolf, the boy projecting himself as a ferocious beast. For the adult Polanski, film offered the opportunity to sketch other self-portraits—but none more poignant than this in *The Tenant*. More than any other major postwar director, Polanski has given us cinema as a drama of identity, a study of self and mask, a performance.

Knife in the Water made Polanski a major East European director, *Repulsion* and *Cul de Sac* established him in the European art cinema, and *Rosemary's Baby* and *Chinatown* did the same in Hollywood. Still Polanski isn't a classic director of the magnitude of Sergei Eisenstein, Jean-Luc Godard, or Alfred Hitchcock, all of whom invented new cinematic possibilities. The contrast with Hitchcock is most relevant, because he and Polanski have probed comparable psychosexual themes. Lacking Hitchcock's sustained aesthetic distance, Polanski has never achieved the lucidity and formal brilliance of *Psycho* or *Rear Window*. Nevertheless, Polanski's disconcerting proximity to his material gives his films their aura of personal risk. Few directors could get away with implicating themselves this directly. Polanski has not changed the art of cinema, but he has managed to use it to remarkably personal ends. This blatant theatricalization of himself on screen gives Polanski his singular but indisputable place in film history.

A Polanski film isn't just a self-contained aesthetic object, for it exists against the vivid background of the director's biographical legend. From the start, as a student at Lodz, he used film to assert the provocative self already sketched in performances and pranks in the Cracow market square. No one else in Poland was making films like *The Crime* or *Break Up the Ball,* indelicate reveries of violence and voyeurism. As in the youthful performances, Romek's strategy for creating a distinctive persona with his films was to step out of the prevailing reality: in this case, forgoing obligatory social and political concerns. The essential Polanskian world was established in the student works, then given greater contour and depth in the feature films.

As an artist of provocation who creates himself through his works, Polanski shares much with Jerzy Kosinski. Like Polanski's films, Kosinski's novels intersect with the public's consciousness of him. Unlike others who suffered the disorientation of the war years, then settled into the relative stability of peacetime, Kosinski and Polanski held on to the perspective afforded by the chaos of war, in which nothing could be taken for granted. The war taught them that social reality is a precarious artifice, capable of crumbling at any moment. This is what Kosinski means when he attributes part of their vision to the war experience. Kosinski and Polanski have walked on the wild side and continue to do so in their art, which explores the limits of unbridled violence and desire.

Kosinski, however, has been the shrewder, for, unlike Polanski, he has accepted the traditional humanistic role of artist as social critic. (Significantly, Kosinski frequently reminds us of his credentials as a trained social scientist.) In the United States he can write about any topic he likes, even hint at his own dark experiences: the seriousness and mission of the social commentator give him the edge to talk openly about the forbidden, the violent, the perverse. Kosinski's novels and interviews suggest a humanism at odds with the actual—and vital—impulse of his art.

Polanski has never had this edge: the social critic's guarantee of seriousness. In his cultivation of immaturity and provocation, Polanski has emulated the great Polish modernist author Witold Gombrowicz, who, in his novel *Ferdydurke*, eschewed the "lofty sentiments and noble thoughts" we expect from artists. (These are precisely the moral guarantees Kosinski has tacked on to his otherwise Gombrowiczian reveries.) Polanski is threatening in the way that children are: we're constantly afraid of what they're going to say or do. The child's amorality has always separated Romek from his audience and accounts for the discomfort Polanski's films often provoke.

After the Manson murders, the amorality associated with Polanski posed problems for him, for he lost control of the image he had created and became a name in the news. To some extent, this loss of control is suffered by any well-known artist whose name and work become independent of him. In the definitive articulation of this experience, Jorge Luis Borges has described seeing his name in print as if it were some other Borges, not himself. But Polanski's case was more extreme, because his name was suddenly associated with events fundamentally unrelated to his art, even though the press and public seemed determined that some link did exist.

Victim of a violent tragedy, Polanski became a participant in a scenario he was no longer directing. After both of the tragedies of his adult life—the murders and the rape case—Polanski made films that imaginatively repeated and reworked those dark events in order to gain mastery over what he had not controlled in reality. Both *Macbeth* and *Tess* evince an obsessive concern with exact period detail —costumes, settings, situations—as if to ensure this mastery.

From *Macbeth* on, Polanski's cinema consistently alludes to a biographical legend, part self-created, part created for him in the mass media. Even relative aesthetic failures like *Macbeth* and *What?* are interesting for the off-screen drama they reflect. Polanski's notorious cameo in so polished a Hollywood product as *Chinatown,* as well as the autobiographical allusions in *The Tenant* and *Tess,* resonate in terms of the public's awareness of Polanski.

The extent of this awareness is incredible. As I researched and wrote this book, many people asked me what I was doing. All of them had something to say about Polanski—shopkeepers, cab drivers, teaching colleagues. Some had never even seen his films aside from the Hollywood standards, *Rosemary's Baby* and *Chinatown.* Had I mentioned some other film director—Alain Resnais or Luchino Visconti, for instance—many of these people would not have had an idea of who they were. But Polanski! Everyone knew Polanski. For all his interest in voyeurism, he may be the cinema's most visible director.

His is a peculiarly modern tale, one possible only in an age of mass media and information. Having set out to create an image for himself—an artistic identity—he became a public effect, to which his art was now pressed to respond.

Polanski's performance has been one of which Romek could never have dreamed.

filmography

DIRECTING CREDITS
SHORT FILMS

The Bicycle [Rower]—1955 (never completed)
The Crime [Morderstwo]—1957
Toothy Smile [Usmiech zębiczny]—1957
Break Up the Ball [Rozbijemy Zabawę]—1958
Two Men and a Wardrobe [Dwaj ludzie z szafą]—1958
The Lamp [Lampa]—1959
When Angels Fall [Gdy spadają anioly]—1959
The Fat and the Lean [Le Gros et le Maigre]—1961
Mammals [Ssaki]—1962

FEATURE FILMS

Knife in the Water [Noz w wodzie]—1962
The Most Beautiful Swindles in the World [Les plus belles escroqueries du monde]—1963—a compilation film with an episode by Polanski called "Amsterdam" or "The Diamond Necklace" [*"La Rivière de diamants"*]
Repulsion—1965
Cul de Sac—1966
The Fearless Vampire Killers or Pardon Me, but Your Teeth Are in My Neck—1967
Rosemary's Baby—1968
Macbeth—1971
What? [Che?]—1973
Chinatown—1974
The Tenant [Le Locataire]—1976
Tess—1979

index

211